T0356658

# COMMITTED

# PRAISE FOR *COMMITTED*

"Sprickerhoff's *Committed* is THE guidebook for aspiring entrepreneurs—being coachable, doing the work, eschewing groupthink, making connections, building a strong team, a compelling offering, good numbers, realizing the importance of sales over investor money, and understanding that money can only solve certain problems. Being prepared for things to fall apart, and being willing to do any job, no matter how small. Seriously loved it!"

Chris Albinson, 5X founder in 3 countries, cofounder
of C100, True North, & CEO of Communitech

"Eldon Sprickerhoff is a legend in the Canadian tech sector -- for his pioneering success in founding eSentire, and also for being one of the best mentors around. Anyone who has ever wanted to start a business will benefit from Eldon's hard-won wisdom, delivered with his usual candor, wit and humility. This is a terrific guide to building great businesses, but also, and maybe even more importantly, it is a book about how to stay sane and hopeful when the going gets tough."

Charles Finlay, Founding Executive Director of Rogers Cybersecure
Catalyst at Toronto Metropolitan University

"Eldon Sprickerhoff's *Committed* is a candid, no-nonsense guide for startup founders, filled with invaluable insights drawn from his own entrepreneurial journey. This book is a goldmine for anyone looking to navigate the often-turbulent waters of building a startup, offering a balanced mix of practical advice and real-life anecdotes that cover the full spectrum of the startup experience—the good, the bad, and the ugly."

Amber French, CEO Catalyst Ventures

"Every successful founder had some kind of competitive advantage. For Eldon, it was his deep experience in cyber defense and a passion for helping companies to protect their data. For first-time entrepreneurs looking to start a high-impact company today, it's *Committed*. Any aspiring or early-stage founder should read this book."

Ross Haleliuk, best-selling author of *Cyber for Builders*

"This is a startup manual written by someone who built a 'unicorn' the old-fashioned way, a lot of hard work and commitment over a long period. The advice is practical and full of information that will help you also understand why things work (or don't work) in a certain way."

Jesse Rodgers, Growth Coach at Communitech and Founder of The Barn

"Refreshingly honest, this book is an invaluable resource for anyone embarking on their entrepreneurial path. Sprickerhoff empowers readers with techniques to not only navigate the challenges, but to embrace them as signs of success. For me, that was liberating and put the wind back in my sails."

Nick Scozzaro, Founder & CEO of ShadowHQ

"In *Committed*, Eldon Sprickerhoff takes us on his personal journey to build a 'unicorn' in the managed detection and response space. Along the way he finds teaching moments, those derived from mistakes, and those that could be termed the basics of startup life. Eldon writes as he lives, compassionately and honestly. Every founder will find value in these pages."

Richard Stiennon, Chief Research Analyst, IT-Harvest,
and author of *Security Yearbook 2024: A History and
Directory of the IT Security Industry* (Wiley, 2024)

"Eldon Sprickerhoff's *Committed* nails the raging battle between euphoria and despair along a founder's journey to success. Eldon's road from zero to $1B puts him in a rare and advantageous position to offer practical insights and strategies that are both profound and accessible. After 20 years of supporting founders and bearing witness to their challenges, *Committed* is one of the most real guides available for anyone truly serious about success as a startup entrepreneur."

Dave Unsworth, cofounder and General Partner
of Information Venture Partners

## Committed (definition)

1. To be dedicated to something
2. To be confined in a psychiatric hospital
3. The state of a formally completed transaction within a relational database management system (RDBMS) that makes all changes visible to other users

# COMMITTED

Startup Survival Tips and Uncommon
Sense for First-Time Tech Founders

## ELDON SPRICKERHOFF

 Sutherland House Experts

TORONTO, 2024

Sutherland House Experts Corporation
260 Heath Street West
Suite 605
Toronto, Ontario
M5P 3L6

First edition, October 2024

Manufactured in the Turkey
Cover designed by Jordan Lunn
Book composed by Karl Hunt

Library and Archives Canada Cataloguing in Publication
Title: Committed : startup survival tips and uncommon sense
for first-time tech founders / Eldon Sprickerhoff.
Names: Sprickerhoff, Eldon, author.
Description: Includes index.
Identifiers: Canadiana (print) 20240436245 | Canadiana (ebook) 20240436253 |
ISBN 9781738396429 (hardcover) | ISBN 9781069039620 (softcover) |
ISBN 9781738396436 (EPUB)
Subjects: LCSH: High technology industries—Management. |
LCSH: New business enterprises—Management.
Classification: LCC HD62.37 .S67 2024 | DDC 620.0068—dc23

Hardcover ISBN 978-1-7383964-2-9
Paperback ISBN 978-1-0690396-2-0
eBook 978-1-7383964-3-6

# Contents

*I have immense empathy for first-time tech founders,
particularly if they don't have specific business acumen.*

---

*You must be a little crazy to start a business.*

---

*You've fallen in love with your offering and want to show
the world so they can fall in love with it too.*

---

*There's so much distance between
ZERO
and
ONE
and so much can go wrong.*

---

*I have written this to encourage you, to help guide
you along the path and recognize your blind spots,
and to learn from my mistakes.*

*I wish to thank my wife and unindicted co-conspirator, Carole,*
*who always knew I would one day write a book.*

# Preface by Ethan Smart

ELDON SPRICKERHOFF AND I met through a mutual friend while I was running my first cybersecurity startup at Black Hat. Bill Dorney (affectionately known as "Dorn Dog") suggested that Eldon could help me understand GTM (Go-To-Market) strategies. Little did I know, Eldon would provide far more than just advice; he would become a mentor and friend, offering guidance that extended well beyond channel strategy.

When Eldon first asked me to read his book, I was three months into my first due diligence process for an acquisition. In my first-time founder ignorance, I was learning one of Eldon's key lessons: "Everything takes longer than you expect. Even when you account for that, it still takes longer." After a grueling three months, I anticipated a signed LOI and cash in the account at any moment. Eldon graciously took many calls from me over the next three additional months as I waited for that LOI.

Eldon repeatedly reminded me of the many lessons he learned, many of which are in his book. His advice is what kept my business and me alive. Primarily, I learned that regardless of what you are working on as a cofounder: coding, negotiating a big sale, talking to potential investors, working on an OEM opportunity, and so on: your sole job is to be nothing less than a Chief Survival Officer. Observing my own journey and those of my peers at many other startups, I realized this is the best hat you could possibly wear.

I cannot stress enough how challenging the journey of a founder is. You may be able to "intellectualize" the difficulty, but until you have experienced the pain, it is impossible to understand. The lessons in this book will help you. The funny thing is, these lessons will help limit the damage like a vaccine. You will find them even more practical in hindsight, and they will help you adjust your course quicker when they are in your mind.

I can promise you that in my own journey, I had to apply each of these lessons. One chapter I highly recommend is "When Things Fall Apart" because, as Matt Damon says in the movie *The Martian*, "At some point, everything's gonna go South on you . . . everything's going to go South and you're going to say, this is it. This is how I end. Now you can either accept that, or you can get to work. That's all it is. You just begin. You do the math. You solve one problem . . . and you solve the next one . . . and then the next."

In my own experience, I managed my company through many difficult waters: COVID-19, Russia's invasion of Ukraine, our bank account being tied up during the crash of Silicon Valley Bank, and our major deals falling apart to a better-funded competitor. The hardest moment was calling Eldon on a Tuesday morning in February 2024 to share the crushing news that the acquisition of my company, after eight months of diligence, was called off. This crushed the personal dreams of myself, my cofounder, and all of our employees. That chapter became a piece of writing I held close to my heart. It was pivotal in guiding myself and my company through the months that followed. This book is worth its weight in not just gold, but the time it will save you as you embark on your startup journey.

And I promise you that even when hard times come or things fall apart, if you listen to Eldon's advice and use it to solve one problem after the next, you will not only survive but also have a much higher chance of achieving your goals and becoming the Chief Thriving Officer of your company. You will manage past the difficult days of holding on and reach a place where you can watch what you've built thrive, just as Eldon is now getting to do with eSentire.

# Prologue

THE DATE IS SEPTEMBER 17, 2017, and I'm walking down 35th Street in Midtown Manhattan with my wife, Carole. We'd spent most of the night at Blue Smoke, a renowned BBQ restaurant in the neighbourhood of Gramercy. The dinner was hosted by eSentire, the company we'd started almost 17 years earlier, but this was unlike any other customer event we'd ever hosted.

After the customer event we went across the street to a basement bar thumping with music, where we drank and danced for a few hours. Then we walked to Han Bat, a favorite twenty-four-hour Korean restaurant. We spent a couple of hours eating *pajeon* (seafood pancakes), *mandu* (dumplings), and kimchi while drinking shots of soju.

Walking back to the hotel, Carole pointed to a clock tower. "Surely it can't be 6:30 a.m.," she says.

And it was. Twenty-four hours ago, we had boarded a plane, and we had not stopped or even slowed down since.

We are celebrating.

September 17 marks a most auspicious day in a few respects. On that day in 2015, we had formally opened eSentire's EU office in Cork, Ireland. And on this date, private equity giant Warburg Pincus would acquire a majority position in our once-tiny company, setting a valuation for eSentire at $150 million USD.

Four years later, with annual recurring revenue in excess of $100 million USD, we had grown to a valuation of $1.1 billion USD—making eSentire respectively both a "centaur" and a "unicorn." The numbers were both dizzying and somewhat bewildering. We had put in a lot of hard miles between the early raw startup days until now.

How did we get here? Certainly owing to some technical competency (if not superiority), coupled with a frenzied urgency to survive and win. And certainly a lot of luck.

But here's what people didn't know then, and most still don't know today. I began my startup journey without a whit of business acumen (other than running a lone wolf consulting shop). Over time, I learned I was coachable and ready to learn. I have had hundreds of fellow employees help to make the company what it is today. I am immensely lucky to have had the opportunity to learn from some of the best in the industry.

So I want to share with you some of what I learned.

A warning: It's not always pretty. But within these pages are stories and advice I'd wish I'd known earlier. And had I known some of them, I might have still needed some luck to get the business to where it is today, just perhaps a lot less of it. And that can make all the difference in maximizing your likelihood of startup survival and business success.

I hope that my stories and advice will inspire you to investigate yourself with care and depth—to honestly examine your capabilities, strengths and weaknesses, and your raw desire to make this endeavor succeed.

Are you ready?

# CHAPTER 1

# Illusory Superiority, Survival, and Harsh Reality

MONG THE HUNDREDS OF cognitive biases observed to afflict the human brain, there's one called "illusory superiority" in which people overestimate their own qualities and abilities when compared to the same qualities and abilities of other people. It is also known as the "above-average" effect and the "superiority bias." Mathematically, we simply cannot all be above average.

Relatedly, within organizational behavior research, there is a similar concept referred to as "self-serving bias." This bias refers to the tendency to believe that successes surface solely from internal factors while failures arise from external factors.

Keeping these biases in mind, consider the well-established fact that most startups don't survive past their first few years in operation, and it is usually not because they were sold to a strategic acquirer and the founder is happily retired on a sunny beach. The overwhelming majority fail outright. Approximately 90 percent of startups fail in the first five years. That is approximately the same odds as playing Russian roulette with five bullets in a six-shot revolver (though not with the same potentially deadly outcome).

When I probed ChatGPT on this matter, it noted that while Russian roulette is a dangerous and potentially deadly game, it should never be played in any circumstances, as the risks of injury or death are high. I recognize that while the odds of playing five-chambered Russian roulette and starting a company are similar, they are not precisely comparable activities inasmuch as the outcomes are markedly dissimilar if you lose.

I find it somewhat difficult to take these broad statistics entirely seriously. It is sometimes the explicit intention of the startup at the outset to only exist for a few years. I presume that it's far likely that a third-time founder who's succeeded during their first two startups will succeed the third time around as opposed to a "green" startup founder. This "90 percent" startup failure data clumps them together clumsily.

Nevertheless, I think these cautionary statistics are useful as a broad characterization: by definition, startups can be remarkably risky. So, keeping the two biases earlier described front of mind, exactly what makes *you* and your startup so special that you believe you can beat those odds?

Since so much can go wrong, even in the startup's first year of existence, let alone at the five-year mark, why do so many entrepreneurs keep trying?

Now that we've acknowledged the risks of startup life, I want to help you beat the odds of survival: to sit well above the depressing statistics described. How am I going to help you do this? For one, I'm going to throw ice-cold water in your face, strip away some of the fantasy and mystique, and awaken you to some of the grim realities of startup life. I particularly like the appropriate analogy of ice-cold water in the face, thanks in great part to the mammalian diving reflex. When you are submerged in cold water, a parasympathetic nervous system response is invoked down to the cellular level. In layman's terms, the parasympathetic nervous system is a part of our body that helps us calm down. Ultimately, this complicated, dynamic, protective, and multifaceted physiologic reaction lowers both your heart rate and blood pressure and creates a calmness designed to help you survive.

The mammalian diving reflex explains a lot about startup survival.

Since starting eSentire in late 2001, I have made dozens of objectively poor decisions. I have been lucky to never have made any single one poor enough to completely sink the ship. I freely admit that plenty of decisions that may have looked like good ideas at the time were, in retrospect, neither well conceived nor well executed. Fortunately, I had (along with the team) made a sufficient number of good decisions—coupled with luck and persistence—to survive and thrive to this point.

---

### TIP FROM THE TRENCHES

*For many years, I've attended a hacker's conference called DEF CON hosted in Las Vegas. When people heard that I was headed to Vegas, they'd ask me if I ever gambled. With a small smile, I'd say that I think they were referring to "gaming," not "gambling." The average gamer in Las Vegas might lose $2K a weekend at the tables or the slots. Yet I was truly gambling as an entrepreneur—I had invested considerable time, money, and my reputation in this startup—such that pretty much my entire life was on the line. Now that was gambling. Losing $2K over a weekend felt like small stakes in comparison. And, for the record, I don't play casino games. Founding a startup can be a big gamble.*

---

So why write this down in a book?

There were at least two good reasons to start this writing project. First, it has been an act of therapeutic catharsis in addressing the past. Second, while working as a mentor at the Rogers Cybersecurity Catalyst—a national center for innovation and collaboration in cybersecurity, headquartered in Brampton, Ontario, and affiliated with Toronto Metropolitan University—I have had the opportunity to share my mishaps one-on-one with founders making some of the same mistakes I did. Plus, there is already no lack of boosterism in the startup world. I didn't want to focus on my successes for without mistakes there are no successes. I want to share the mistakes I had made so that first-time founders could sidestep them. By learning from my mistakes, they could then go on their path to make their own, perhaps novel, and exciting mistakes! I want first-time founders to make mistakes, just not the same ones I did. I would like you to become a "mistake innovator," learning from your inevitable setbacks and not to be afraid of them.

My hope is that these anecdotes inspire and perhaps even scare you a bit. I hope that they will help you look past the swagger and hype of *TechCrunch* articles about the glories of startup culture and face head-on the often harsh realities of startup life. I hope that you will realize that I (among many others) have walked the very same path through which you're currently traveling. I am trying to share with you the many traps and pitfalls ahead so that you can be mindful and avoid them.

I would like you, as a new founder, to bravely take on yet another title: that of the "Chief Survival Officer." Focus on your insanity (for people *will* call you insane), embrace your passion, lead your agile team, and prepare to do what it takes to *survive*.

And if you think that this reality is a bit too grim, perhaps you're not ready to make this journey quite yet. And that's perfectly OK as well. But, if my simple words are all that it took for you to abandon your journey, you need to review your level of commitment. It is going to get a lot rockier. Reality is discouraging sometimes, but only by knowing what commitment means can you see that reality and course bravely through it.

# CHAPTER 2

# Core Startup Truths

*"The scars you share become lighthouses for other people who are headed to the same rocks you hit."*

—Jon Acuff, author of *Finish: Give Yourself the Gift of Done* and *Soundtracks: The Surprising Solution to Overthinking*

I F YOU'RE READING THIS BOOK, you may be considering life as an entrepreneur. Are you thinking about quitting your job? Becoming a contractor? Starting a company with a brilliant idea you've been mulling over for months? Or perhaps you are already in the earliest stages of an independent endeavor, looking forward to the adventures ahead.

Congratulations!

To help you in your journey, I would like to tell you this:

Running a startup is the hardest thing I've ever done. I compare it to raising a child: the effort that goes toward a successful conception is much more fun and considerably easier than the first ten years of the actual upbringing. Starting a company takes little more than an afternoon of enthusiastic effort. The years ahead of continual care and feeding of this creation are what is truly difficult.

## PERSONAL CASE STUDY:
## LONE WOLF TO COFOUNDER

*Before starting eSentire, I had been working on contract gigs as a "lone wolf consultant." I had found one very good and steady contract at a prime brokerage in New York City in early 2000, commuting back home to Canada every weekend. But after the birth of our daughter in mid-2001, thanks to a global recession on the heels of the dot-com and the "dot-bomb" eras and to the dreadful events of 9/11, that contract was facing its ending. Both my (incredibly patient and supportive) wife and I decided that it was definitely time to come back home and start a new chapter.*

*All I knew how to do by then were defense tactics and techniques employed within the somewhat niche field of information security. I had some definite advantages not available to all: At thirty-four years of age, I was healthy and, though young, had accumulated significant experience on my CV. I had a very good network from years of consulting and working in different environments for a range of companies. I was proud of the work that I had done, and, importantly, I had a good reputation. From my previous contract work, we had been fortunate and had saved enough money so that we had almost entirely paid off our house. I knew what it took from a "hustle" perspective to run a one-man consulting business and knew that I could always do that again if needed.*

*Before my contract in New York City ended, I had met with Edmund Dengler over several weekends. Edmund was a long-time childhood friend—we had met* on the second day of first grade. Our lives had overlapped and shared an arc: we were together in public school and high school, completing computer science degrees in university, and we even collaborated on some small consulting gigs afterward. He was currently working on his PhD program at the University of Waterloo but was interested in some ideas for starting a company of some type. For several weeks, we floated some ideas at Tim Horton's coffee shops. We settled on starting an information security company that would deploy the tactics and techniques I had honed by defending hedge funds against cyber threats while working at the prime brokerage.

To help cushion any concerns with our cash flow, my wife and I agreed to take a $150K line of credit against the family home to launch the company and ensure that we had a liquidity cushion upon which we could rely to ride out the waves of uncertainty. It was a huge risk, and I didn't want to contemplate what would happen if it failed. We were united in our efforts to make this work. We all knew that we could "live lean" for quite a while (meaning no extravagances including vacations or new vehicles).

I recognize that not everyone contemplating a startup has these same significant advantages. I had a cofounder whom I knew very well and could trust to be as committed to the goals of the company as I was. I had a tremendously supportive wife who dedicated her time and diligence to doing the bookkeeping for the new company. Further, we had some early ideas regarding some information security services we could offer; plus we already had a network of potential clients.

But we goofed in our planning: we didn't really do any cost-benefit analyses. Nor did we work through the pros and cons of starting a business.

When we started eSentire, I was too foolish not to know that it couldn't work. If ignorance were breakfast cereal, we'd have been based in Battle Creek, Michigan, home to Kellogg's Cereal City and the annual National Cereal Festival. We were foolish, blind, and out of touch with reality.

There's one thing I've found common among first-time founders: if you didn't start out with the most optimistic view, with the rosiest of rose-colored glasses, you would never begin. The saying, "You don't need to be crazy to work here, but it helps," absolutely, definitely, positively applies to the startup world. You need to have at least a bit of crazy (aka intrepid) optimism. The word "committed" has two meanings that are apropos to starting your endeavor. First, you will need to commit yourself to the generously unglamorous realities of startup life. Second, if you really thought about the dismal aspects of startup life and *still* decided to jump in, maybe you are a little mentally unwell and your friends and family need to have you committed.

To that point, I want to introduce several sobering facts about startup life:

First, you'd better love what you do. And, I mean, you must seriously *love it*. You must be wholly besotted by it. If you regard starting a company as a means to an end—like "get rich quick" or "get rich"—it is probably not going to work out for you. When you consider startup failure rates, there are many easier, faster, and more consistent ways to simply make money. Thanks to Professor Larry Smith for this specific piece of advice given to me in his ECON 101 class back in 1987. Larry Smith is well known among the greater University of Waterloo student body for having taught 10 percent of all alumni, his TedX talk, "Why You Will Fail to Have a Great Career," and his book *No Fears, No Excuses*, where he argues that you must have true passion for your work in order to achieve any measure of success. It might be the most valuable thing he ever said. I take it to heart and hope you will, too.

Second, if you build a better mousetrap, the world will not simply beat a path to your front door. Even though you fall in love with your product, solution, offering, and new company, it is practically a given that nobody else will feel quite the same *coup de foudre*. You will need to make sure that your love does not blind you to the shortcomings of your wonderful mousetrap. You might also discover that your better mousetrap can't solely sustain a company. By this, I mean that I have seen many companies built from university "capstone projects" that were in fact better suited to be features of a larger product. Only through ego and sheer force of will did the founders mold and pressure these projects into a tortured corporate existence. These projects don't usually survive as standalone companies in the long term. But that is often fine. After a few years of existence, a good number of these are considered ideal targets for acquisition by larger and generally somewhat moribund companies (aka "strategic acquirers"). This might be exactly what you're hoping for, and if so, you need to focus your efforts on ensuring this outcome takes place within a specific time frame.

To that end . . .

Third, everything will take longer than you expect. Everything. Much. Longer. That includes signing contracts, hiring employees, building and refining new products, raising capital, and more.

Third Prime, I repeat (this gets two mentions for emphasis)! Everything will take longer than you expect, even when you *expect* it to take longer and you take that into account. Reread the previous bullet. You will need to accept this as fact and dedicate yourself to the startup process for it to survive and for you to succeed. Given this, are you ready to do what you need to do to survive?

Third Prime Two, when things do "click" with your startup, be prepared for things to happen faster than you are prepared for (previous two points notwithstanding). You may find yourself caught in a cyclical motion of feast or famine, drought or flood.

Fourth, if, at the beginning, you haven't fully committed yourself to your startup, treating it as a side hustle is fine. Especially if you don't have sufficient capital to make it a full-time endeavor, a side hustle is a superb way to test the water and see if there is sufficient appetite in the market, determine early product-market fit, figure out appropriate pricing, and so many other details. More importantly, you might discover that you enjoy it as a hobby but not as a full-time commitment. It's best to find that out earlier. However, if it becomes successful, at some point, you'll need to make a commitment and dedicate yourself to Plan A: put all your eggs into one basket, carefully guard that basket, and actively fight anyone who threatens the basket or its hatchlings.

Fifth: All of the easy work has already been done. What do I mean by this? If someone looks at a task ahead and says, "Oh, that's easy," you can bet that it is not the case. If it were truly easy, it would likely have been done already. As an example, your predecessors did the heavy lifting necessary to build out the architecture and implementation of the internet. You don't need to build it yourself, so looking back it probably looks easy (and possibly obvious). That was not the case. All your future projects and successes will not be easy; you will need to do the heavy lifting. When you pivot or refine your offering, you'll look back on your original effort and think that was the easy part as well.

11

Sixth: The longer you survive in business, the more you *should* become aware of your blind spots. You don't know everything about everything; at some point, you'll need to humbly acknowledge the gaping maw of your ignorance, especially if you achieve some measure of success. Beware of those early successes as they may lead to even more self-serving bias. Having a skeptical outsider call you on your own self-served bull-crap can help.

Seventh: Because you have a huge project ahead of you, and you have massive blind spots, you probably can't do it alone. You might need to find a cofounder. Ideally you will be able to find someone who's sufficiently aligned with your plans. It demands a partner both committed to taking the risk a startup entails for some unknown amount of time and who can complement your knowledge and personality gaps. This is as important as choosing your spouse. Perhaps it *is* your spouse. Also keep in mind that no matter how well you know and trust your cofounder, make sure that the corporate structure (e.g., cap table, founders shares, vesting schedule) is detailed in a contract.

Eighth: At the early stages, mere survival should be considered success. Perhaps a dozen factors will come into play before you find some significant and real measure of success. These could include timing, market demand, product fit, competition, pricing, macroeconomic conditions, and luck. Depending on your definition of success, hard work isn't likely going to be enough. Luck may eventually come your way, but you'll need to survive long enough for it to find you.

Ninth: You will not be able to abdicate the responsibility to manage the sales process. The reason being simple economics: you might not be able to afford someone else. You will need to get comfortable pitching your offering as a basic part of the sales process. You will need to build a platform upon which you can broadcast the virtues of your product offering. If you are an avowed introvert (as I am), you will need to find the courage inside of you to get out there, get comfortable with being uncomfortable, and *sell*. Your company will not survive if you don't. Perhaps you will find a cofounder or another trusted advisor or partner that has sales experience and acumen to assist you to fill your own gaps. As a founder, even if you designate someone else to oversee sales, early in the existence of your company, sales are likely to fall wholly on you.

Tenth: You will need to generate revenue to survive. Cash flow is probably the best indicator of a business' ability to survive long term, and as much as it is not particularly sexy, actual earned revenue is far more valuable than external funding. There are too many examples of companies that raised external capital but couldn't back it up with actual revenue. I look at Element.AI as a specific fairly recent example. Significant capital raises may make for good headlines and entries in *Crunchbase* and win the admiration of others in your peer group or accelerator, but capital is just a tool. Before setting up your company consider the broader economic opportunities available to you, including tax exclusion zones, potential funding available through government sources, and special capital gains treatment. Few first-time founders take this into consideration, but I guarantee that successful first-time founders, upon starting their second endeavor, definitely consider potentially tax advantageous domiciles and long-term capital gains structures available to them (including but not exclusive to trusts). Do not assume that your presently-domiciled location is the best to incorporate and start your business.

The ten-plus-two commandments I've presented are daunting. Is that enough cold water splashed in your face? Do you feel your heart rate settle? Is your breathing calm?

You might have thought that this bit of writing was meant to be inspirational, and here I am, coming across as a serious buzzkill to your startup dreams. I don't mean to be. I want you to know that there are many reasons that the vast majority of startups don't appear to survive past that infamous five-year milestone. There are times of feast and famine within the startup communities, and macroeconomic factors outside of your control can swing your fate: in late 2022 and early 2023, access to investment capital was tighter than in the previous year due to the vicissitudes of the global economy. The pendulum swings back and forth, which is all the more reason why I don't want you to make the same mistakes I did. I want you to maximize your chances.

Being excited about starting a new business just isn't going to be enough when the grind starts. At times, I've described a startup's journey as being akin to having your first child. It is very exciting, new, and fun at the beginning—everybody is congratulating you, and you're truly at the beginning of something that feels momentous and perhaps more than a little overwhelming with high expectations. After the baby is born, along with the fanatical highs of parenthood, there are the lows of sleepless nights, exhaustion, dirty diapers, and sickness—a departure from what you may have expected when you first had that great idea. It is going to take a lot to get you through the startup slog.

## TIP FROM THE TRENCHES: MENTORS MAY SHOW UP WHERE YOU LEAST EXPECT

*Dave Beer is a gentleman you likely won't find presenting a keynote at any conference. He is not on LinkedIn, the business networking platform. He is as far outside the tech community as any entrepreneur business owner could be. However, I received plentiful servings of excellent business advice from him early in my journey. Dave runs a small commercial cleaning company; I first met him while he was cleaning other units in our first office building.*

*In addition to being a very industrious guy, Dave is both quite chatty and friendly. As we were both working late in the office (after most other tenants in the building had gone home), we had an excellent opportunity to get to know each other better. We talked about our own radical optimism upon starting our ventures, in addition to the cold reality of the grind.*

*Dave became what might at first glance be considered an unexpected early mentor.*

*At the beginning, he had many more employees than we had; I had asked his advice for balancing headcount and workload. He gave astute advice because he had many years of managing employees, balancing workload, while consistently delivering a quality offering.*

*Among the hiring advice he gave me was to always be looking for terrific employees. Do not assume that any single employee will stay with you for a specific amount of time. You must recognize where you fit into their lifetime career plans. No matter how good any single employee is, do not become reliant on any one employee for a specific task. Ensure there is no single point of failure.*

*Eventually, as we grew, I was able to return the favor to him. The mentee could become the mentor!*

*One night he asked me, "Eldon, I have some great clients. Let's say that I have a contract to vacuum and take out the garbage at the end of every workday. From time to time, a client's office manager will call me up and ask for some small additional service. For example, they'll ask if I can clean the microwave as well. The unspoken assumption is that I can take care of this small request with no additional cost. How do I handle this delicately?"*

*I told him that in technology, we have a project management term for this very situation. It is known as "Scope Creep." My advice: "Gladly and assertively say 'I can do that. Let me get you a quote.'"*

*This establishes a framework: it sets the scene that the request is not included in the current cost and gives them the opportunity to decline that option. Every time any current client asks for an additional service, immediately say "yes," but also state that it will require an additional charge.*

*I told him, "You have already established a business relationship with them; they are pleased with the arrangement and are asking for more services. Your services provide demonstrable value to them. If you give services away for free, you have implicitly devalued your value in their eyes, and they will keep coming back to you with additional requests at the same zero-cost price point. You need to value yourself to avoid that slippery slope."*

*I give this same advice to many founders. Value yourself and your offering.*

---

Embarking on a startup is exciting, but there are some harsh realities that you will need to face—better sooner than later. When the student is ready, the teacher will surface: mentors may show up when you least expect it.

# CHAPTER 3

# The Will to Survive

THERE'S AN OLD (well, old in internet years) *Slashdot* article often referred to as the "Missing Steps Plan," which is no longer archived online. In my own case, when starting eSentire, my "missing steps plan" looked something along the lines of this:

1. Start an info-security firm, with specific focus on a "managed services" offering
2. ???
3. Profit!

There's a lot that's missing in step 2: The "black hole" of getting the right stuff done. Within the mentorship work I've led in the last five years, too often I find this to be the default case. Sometimes there's a seed of an idea but not a plan or even the slightest idea of how to get to step 3. The founders I meet have often fallen in love with their idea and are not able to pivot to get the perspective of a potential client or partner. Are you flexible enough, with enough capacity for introspection, to recognize this?

Ideally, a "tried and true" blueprint for success as taught in business school normally looks like this:

1. Identify your passion
2. Do your market research
3. Test hypotheses and hold off on too-rapid expansion
4. Set fixed goals
5. Have a long-term exit strategy

There's nothing wrong with this theoretical approach, but from what I've seen (and personally experienced), most startups are so engaged in their battle for survival that their founders do not have the capacity to follow such a rigid blueprint.

To be fair, that isn't necessarily their fault. Sometimes there is too much emphasis put on building a formal business plan as though it is an MBA capstone project. This is the difference between "in theory" and "in practice."

This blueprint does not automatically consider the harsher realities of the situation. It does not show what Pink Floyd popularized as "dark side of the moon"—the unknown unknowns—or how much iceberg is hidden beneath the water. You can build a beautiful business plan that would get you the highest honors in your MBA class but may never survive the rough and tumble daily reality since that business plan cannot possibly describe 90 percent of the headwinds you will be facing. For this reason, when setting strategic startup plans, I believe it is better to adhere to Jeff Bezos' concept of "strong convictions, loosely held."

This chapter's goal is to provide a small peek behind the glossy promise of the "startup life" to prepare founders for the reality of the early grind. Without the will to keep going, you will not survive the myriad difficulties ahead, many unknown. It is not enough to simply love what you do. It is a cold, harsh truth: the broader market itself doesn't care about your company or your passion or even you! Eventually, you will discover that aside from early friends-and-family investment rounds, your investors don't really care about you—their primary goal is to make a massive return on their investment.

Never mind. Keep grinding.

## HOW DO YOU IDENTIFY YOUR PASSION AND WHO WILL PAY FOR YOU TO PURSUE IT?

As I've said earlier, Professor Larry Smith has written an excellent book on how to have an exceptional career. It is not merely enough to find something that you are passionate about. At the core of it, you need to find the *Ikigai* focus: the Venn diagram where "What You Are Good At," "What You Love to Do," and "What Will People Pay For" intersect.

If you are lucky, you might discover there are a few items that fall inside that intersection. Even if you are lucky enough to find one excellent candidate, there's good reason for significant optimism.

If, at the very beginning, you weren't wildly optimistic about your future prospects—and I mean stupidly optimistic, insanely optimistic, bubbling over with relentless and unbridled optimism—you would never start a company. For all the excitement that you might feel, the reality is not typically glamorous, especially during those fateful first five years. It is usually a brutish grind, with burned shoe leather and sweat-soaked business travel in economy plane seats and terrible hotels. Surviving the first five years is something like the last five miles of a first marathon—an exercise in what I call "The Will."

You will need to dig deep inside and find The Will to push on. You will need to push yourself in ways you hadn't originally conceived.

## HOW MUCH RESEARCH DO YOU NEED BEFORE YOU LAUNCH?

As a bootstrapped or self-financed startup founder, how do you decide how to get started? Later in this book, I will discuss the need for a minimally viable product (MVP), but at the beginning, you need to start with a core idea: a seed that could conceivably grow into an MVP. Does this offering already exist? What gaps currently exist in the solutions offered by your potential competitors? Just because you yourself don't know about it doesn't mean that someone else isn't already executing on a similar idea.

I recommend that you reach out throughout your network (you've been building your LinkedIn profile, right?) and see if you can get referrals to people who have experience bringing something like your idea to the market. It is critical not to merely bounce ideas off your own echo chamber.

There's no need to perform an exhaustive market research study. I do recommend that you survey the surrounding horizon before committing to this passion project.

## MY FIRST SIGNIFICANT CLIENT

*The first significant client we signed was located in Manhattan; it happened serendipitously. Many months before, in early 2001, an early internet service provider (or ISP) by the name of Pilot Networks went bankrupt and shuttered. Its customers were given a week's grace period to move to a new provider. At the prime brokerage where I was doing contract work, we had a plan to migrate firewalls away from Pilot to a new ISP on Saturday morning. However, a separate business unit to the prime brokerage's parent company (the investment management arm) was also using Pilot Networks and needed help to move over to the new ISP. They didn't have a firewall technician on staff and were looking for someone who could assist. I said that I could do it, but it would have to take place on Sunday morning.*

*By the end of Sunday morning, I had made the appropriate firewall changes and thoroughly tested all of the connections. The entire process had taken about three hours. I billed $240 USD for my work. The VP was so pleased with my work that he and his staff took me out for Asian cuisine at TAO in Midtown Manhattan, a fashionable three-floor-level restaurant boasting a skybox private dining room and a second-floor mezzanine. I'm sure the dinner bill was more than what I billed for the firewall migration work.*

*But from this single event, I had established a work ethic, reliability, fair pricing, and most importantly, trust. Even after that original contract at the prime brokerage had finished, that same VP reached out to me for small pieces of contract work that he needed completed. There was one point where he asked me what my thoughts were for the future. I described to him what I was thinking regarding an information security services firm, and he told me that he wanted to be our first customer.*

*Ultimately, he became one of our best "alpha" clients; he was willing to go along with us on whatever crazy security idea we had, acting as a mentor, a cheerleader, and a reference. From this humble $240 consulting gig, an international cybersecurity powerhouse with a future billion-dollar enterprise value was born. But this trajectory was over twenty years in the making.*

You will need to make yourself known in your specialized community as a thought leader. Equipped with social media, it is easier than ever for you to get your voice out into the community. However, consistency is key to maintaining eyeballs. There are hundreds of blogs, LinkedIn campaigns, and podcasts that had their genesis with the best of intentions and eventually fell into stasis. I strongly recommend that you trumpet your own research and findings. Submit talks to every applicable conference you can, especially if you are speaking to your target client base. You might not be able to be accepted to headline large conferences. Never mind: there are dozens of smaller conferences at which you can cut your teeth and become more comfortable. We will discuss some of these techniques further in the demand generation/filling-the-sales-funnel section of this book.

Building on the early successes we had in New York City, I submitted proposals for talks at conferences worldwide, putting myself out there on the public stage. I was not particularly comfortable with public speaking, but I recognized that if we were to survive it wasn't going to happen without my using every avenue of outreach available.

## IMPOSTER PHENOMENON

*This is as good a time as any to discuss imposter phenomenon (IP) or what is often erroneously referred to as imposter syndrome. Drs. Pauline Rose Clance and Suzanne Imes first coined the term "imposter phenomenon" to describe people who feel that their successes are due to "lucky breaks" and not the result of their own innate ability and competence. To this day, Dr. Clance expresses distaste with the fact that it is popularly known as a "syndrome" rather than a "phenomenon." There exist proven methods for people to help address their feelings of imposter phenomenon and exert mastery over their mindsets.*

*There will always be someone more accomplished than you, but you can help to share your ideas and knowledge with those who are hungry to learn.*

Once you plant this seed and begin this journey, the entire process will take more time, money, and consistent effort than you originally thought. I have not seen "overnight success" without a bedrock of time, money, and effort invested upfront. Many years ago, I often joked with people saying that I was working "half days," meaning twelve hours a day, seven days a week. Even Jack Ma of Alibaba fame has made famous his "996" work week, being 9 a.m.—9 p.m., six days a week, leading to a 72-hour work week. If this is what is needed to ultimately succeed, do you have it in you?

I would add one caveat: don't work crazy hours merely because of what I've said—work thoughtfully, effectively, with the outcome in mind. Over the course of weeks and months (and even years!) you're likely more effective working eight supremely focused hours a day than twelve lackluster hours.

At the earliest days of your startup, your very survival is paramount and not at all guaranteed. Don't hold too tightly to any single rigid strategy. At the beginning, it is unlikely that you know exactly what the market wants, or what it will do with the solution you've presented. Don't expect that a rigid business plan will survive the buffeting winds of uncertainty on any given day.

For every person truly supportive of your effort, there are many more who are laughing at you (mostly in private, but some even to your face). I am reminded of what Babe Ruth said—"the loudest boos are from the cheapest seats"—or William Safire's "nattering nabobs of negativism." Nobody likes to be laughed at. You will need to dig deep and push on despite your detractors.

Do you have it in you to push through discomfort? It has been said that you will need to get comfortable with being uncomfortable. For me, a self-professed introvert, I discovered early on in my entrepreneurial journey that clients weren't going to make their way to us—I would need to go out there and find them. Before we had any salespeople, sales leader was one of the several hats I wore: the burned shoe leather to which I referred earlier is my own.

When you're pitching your offering, you'll need to become comfortable with vulnerability. Sales is the act of vulnerability embodied. You'll need to become comfortable with less-than-enthusiastic prospects. You'll need to be able to answer the question: "*So what?*"

Other than a famous Miles Davis jazz composition, what is "*So what?*"

Let's say that you're pitching your product or service offering. The potential clients are listening intently, and after you're finished, the one most bookish raises her hand, and she says, "*So what?*"

"*So what?*"

This is one of those questions that could be a knockout blow if you're not ready for it. Don't take it personally. You'll need to be prepared for these curveballs throughout and even beyond your startup-to-scale-up journey.

First, don't be defensive. Take a deep breath. You need to consider every outbound discussion you have as an opportunity for valuable feedback to help you improve.

Second, do not immediately jump to answer the question specifically. Try to enable a dialogue by asking questions in response.

Third, use their skepticism to hone both your pitch and response to prepare for the future.

To that end, you'll need to get used to getting your heart broken, repeatedly. You'll need to get used to being knocked down, repeatedly. There is no doubt that luck plays a significant part of your journey to success—can you survive until luck strikes? I am often reminded of why there are so many excellent restaurants in Manhattan. Starting a restaurant in Manhattan is at least as daunting as any tech-focused entrepreneurial startup: there's a crowded market of competitors, fussy clients, outrageous expenses, and difficult circumstances. If you're to start a successful restaurant in Manhattan, you will need to quickly find your balance, gain happy, and repeat customers ("regulars"), or else there will be an excited line of others ready to rent the space once you've left.

Without The Will to keep going, you will not survive the myriad difficulties before you. It is not enough to simply love what you do.

In order to survive, you will need to steel yourself for objections, some ruder than others.

Have a calm, assured, and engaged process ready for prime time when a belligerent or inscrutable potential client asks, "So what?"

# CHAPTER 4

# VUCA and a World of Volatility, Uncertainty, Complexity, and Ambiguity

W E LIVE IN A VUCA world—one rife with volatility, uncertainty, complexity, and ambiguity.

The acronym, VUCA, traces to 1987, based on the leadership theories of Warren Bennis and Burt Nanus. I was introduced to the VUCA framework in 2016 during an offsite management course held by the Thayer Leadership Group at West Point. We were discussing some of the inherent difficulties in business execution, and the VUCA framework was presented. This was a profoundly enlightening experience for me.

We have, I feel, always lived in a VUCA environment, and it seems that as of late it has reached even more of a fever pitch. The easiest example to detail could be the capital markets. Consider the frothy and exuberant capital markets of 2018 through to 2020, the financial shocks to the system due to COVID-19 lockdowns, the world's central banks flooding the market with cheap capital, and the inflation spike. This mix of system shocks culminated in corresponding and drastic increases in the prime lending rate. As a result, in early 2023, the pendulum of the capital markets swung back. It was, suddenly, a considerably more difficult time to raise capital for early-stage founders.

> *What made this VUCA world especially germane to my business is that VUCA is itself core to the value of a cybersecurity offering. Without even knowing it, we had stumbled into it: our service offered the market a product that helped to address and mitigate the threats lurking on the internet. Volatile, because no two days were exactly the same from an attack perspective. Uncertain, because there was no obvious way to understand attacks and the underlying internet traffic. Complex, because many attackers were sophisticated in ways that our clients were not. Ambiguous, because it was not immediately clear how to defend and respond.*
>
> *The broader market was not ready for our solution in 2001, but by 2008, there was an appetite for it.*

If the market is not ready for what you're selling, you need to take business advantage of that reality and own it. First, you need to realize that you may truly be so far ahead of the curve that you'll need to seek out early adopters and educate them. This will take considerable time and effort, but you may find that you have no competition.

In academic business circles, this is called a Blue Ocean Strategy (as opposed to Red Ocean). Created by INSEAD professors of strategy, W. Chan Kim and Renée Mauborgne, the Blue Ocean strategy refers to a business universe that must be created because it does not yet exist, as opposed to an established business universe rife with competitors and well-established product offerings (where the ocean runs red with blood). The strategic benefit of finding your place within a Blue Ocean is that if you survive long enough, you may find yourself to be the standard against which clients and experts judge all competitors in your market.

*In the early aughts, there wasn't a lot of competition in the managed security space for two reasons. First, the dot-bomb implosion of the late 1990s had wiped out many tech startups. Second, the market demand wasn't quite there yet. Cyberattacks were not sufficiently painful to the broader community; there was, therefore, little awareness that there were serious threats to be mitigated and problems to be solved. It was an almost perfect Blue Ocean scenario.*

I don't have a formal academic business degree, but I hope you're starting to see that there are some excellent principles that I believe apply to the startup world well beyond cybersecurity, especially when you're trying to define your own offering. My travels as a tech founder to client events and conferences around the world reinforce these principles, for it's often through observation of others that we can best see ourselves.

# CHAPTER 5

# "O Wad Some Pow'r the Giftie Gie Us to See Oursels as Ithers See Us!"

THIS PROSE FRAGMENT FROM Robbie Burns translates as follows: "Oh would some power the gift to give us, to see ourselves as others see us. It would save us from many mistakes and foolish thoughts, we would change the way we look and gesture."

This premise is universal. Case in point: let's move from Scotland to Japan.

Within Yoshinkan Aikido, a Japanese martial art that features joint locks, throws, and pins against opponents, there is a construct called "Shite Uke Kotai" in which the person who was previously "executing" the technique changes places with the person who was "receiving" the technique.

Throughout your startup journey you will need to put yourself into the other person's shoes. This will apply to fellow employees, possible clients, investors, and, in fact, pretty much everyone whom you may encounter during your mission. The earlier you assess the motivations of others, the more successful you will be in your journey. Ask yourself questions intentionally: *Why* would someone want to join your small company when other larger, ostensibly more secure options are available? *Why* would a potential client want to risk their comfortable employment to incorporate your offering into their enterprise? *Why* would an investor risk their reputation, their own post-taxed personal capital, and the capital of their limited partners to invest in your risky company?

At the core of our being, I believe that we are not terribly complicated animals: in some ways, we are barely evolved troglodytes. Our underlying programming (or "wetware") has not been significantly updated. One interpretation of the late American psychologist Abraham Maslow's *Hierarchy of Needs* states that we are motivated by (among others) fear, greed, sex, status, and survival. Though we aren't defending ourselves from saber-tooth tigers today, we are in competition with each other. Your potential clients are fearful of losing their jobs, their place in society, and the admiration of their peers and are even fearful for their solvency and resilience.

On a deeper level, to elaborate on Maslow's somewhat crude hierarchy, other people's motivations may include a subset of these eleven dimensions:

- Altruism
- Autonomy
- Competition
- Feedback
- Financial needs
- Innovation
- Progress
- Rationality
- Security
- Social relationships
- Status

As the Chief Survival Officer, you will need to consider others' specific motivations in order for you, and your startup, to survive.

It, therefore, behooves you to consider your customers' viewpoint and elemental needs and let these help guide you through the customer journey with positioning and sales. Consider your fellow employees' specific motivations. Helping to fulfill those needs will help you to build a stronger company.

# CHAPTER 6

# Defining and Building Your Brand

**A**T THE EARLIEST STAGES of a startup, there's little differentiation between your personal brand and the brand of the startup itself. Perhaps unfairly, your reputation, previous work, history, and interactions among your broader network are all imprinted on your startup.

That said, there are many effective grassroots means by which you can position yourself as the firm's brand ambassador (yet another hat you need to wear). It will require somewhat of a formal communication process. Though you might find it painful and frankly unnecessary, I guarantee that it is critical to your eventual success. You will need to establish a regular cadence of outreach to establish credibility to the community at large, including potential employees, customers, and investors. As well, you will need to establish a separate (yet still regular) cadence of communication to update existing employees, customers, and current investors and board members.

At the earliest stages (before you have minted community credibility), you should focus on establishing yourself as a thought leader. This will require curated content. I suggest that on a regular basis (say, weekly), you isolate some facet of the problem that you're solving and assemble a cogent analysis. LinkedIn and X (née Twitter) are the two media platforms that I expect can help you build a grassroots following and help establish domain expertise; perhaps someday TikTok or some other currently unknown competitor will unseat them.

Unless you have domain-specific expertise in marketing, do not simply do it yourself. Find a marketing professional with specific expertise in your offering and enlist them in helping to build your brand and create and reach your audience. Shoddy marketing efforts will win you no clients.

## A CAVEAT ABOUT OUTSOURCING
## OF PR AND MARKETING

*Early in the beginning of eSentire, we were struggling with messaging and realized that we needed some assistance with marketing our offering. We were referred by one of our clients (in the hedge fund/alternative asset management sector) to an agency in Manhattan that catered specifically to that vertical. We met with the principal; he was a former football player with an imposing presence and build. He eagerly described the unquestionable and direct access he had to over a hundred hedge fund CTOs, to whom he could make introductions and referrals on our behalf.*

*His terms were simple: First, we would pay a fee of six thousand US dollars per month to his company. Second, if we sold anything through the connections his company made, they would get a twenty-point commission. And if, after a year, there was success, he would have the ability to take an early equity position in our company. We didn't immediately turn him down; we asked for some evidence of his ability to sell services—key performance indicators (KPIs) and a few key customer references—and we said that we would need to do some due diligence.*

*We had several clients already in common with the PR agency so we did some low-key due diligence questions. Questions included, "How long have you known this person?" "How did you meet them?" "What do his outreach events or efforts look like?" and "Have you ever purchased anything through them?"*

*We felt these questions were innocuous, but the answers were remarkable in what they revealed. Among all of the references he gave us, only one had purchased a single item due to his introduction, and that was some server RAM that was discounted in price. He had never sold services, only products. Why, then, would over 100 hedge fund CTOs pick up the phone when he called?*

*We learned that several times a year, he would book a box at Yankee Stadium or Madison Square Gardens and invite the CTOs to see a game at his expense. That was it. Yankee Stadium was apparently a particular favorite.*

*When we went back to visit him, he asked if we were going to engage his company. I said, "You've described the pricing as follows—and I want to make sure that I heard it correctly. First, you'll get a monthly charge. Second, you'll get a commission on every sale that comes as part of the introduction. Third, if this business relationship works out well, you'll get the chance to take an equity position in the company. Correct?" He confirmed my understanding.*

*I replied, "To me that feels like you're going to want a piece of cake, and you'll want to grab some of my cake as well, and while you're munching on both portions, you're going to want me to give you a reach around."*

*He did not know what to say to that. He didn't tell me that I was wrong, though.*

*I noted that I hadn't received those KPIs I had asked for; he said that he would send them, and we made our exit. You should be unsurprised to hear that we never received the sales KPIs he had promised, and ultimately, we chose not to work with his firm.*

*This doesn't mean that you shouldn't look for external help. It took us more time, research, and effort but eventually we found a much better, more professional external team. Don't assume that the first one you meet (even if it is a referral from a so-called trusted source) is the right one. The lights of Yankee Stadium can blind some people.*

If you're better acquainted with some of the mechanisms of marketing, you'll be able to make better decisions regarding what team might provide the best fit to close the missing gaps. At this stage of your business, you will need to distinguish at least three key disciplines of marketing: demand generation, lead generation, and referral automation. Demand generation is simply the process and motion behind educating the market about the specific problems you solve. If you are in the "Blue Ocean" territory where there are no immediate or obvious competitors, it is likely that you will need to devote significant time and effort to educating your potential client base. Lead generation is the process by which you engage potential customers to qualify them for your sales funnel. Finally, referral automation is the process of so delighting your customers that they, in turn, act as agents for you to educate the market on your behalf, creating a "flywheel" of demand generation and lead generation themselves. In later chapters, we will dig deeper into this marketing and sales journey.

Your personal brand, your startup's brand, and your associated company mission will be critical in your ability to get people interested or even excited about your startup. While you will be the standard bearer for the company, you're probably not going to be able to do this alone, so we should talk about those who are going to go along on this journey with you: your fellow employees.

At the earliest stages of your startup, your own reputation and personal brand will be tantamount to its success. Prepare by setting yourself up for marketing its success.

# CHAPTER 7

# Your Fellow Travelers on This Journey

**MEN WANTED**

for hazardous journey, small wages,

bitter cold, long months of complete

darkness, constant danger. Safe return

doubtful, honor and recognition

in event of success.

—Ernest Shackleton

THERE IS SOME DEBATE whether Ernest Shackleton, the famed explorer of Antarctica, took out this ad seeking recruits. But its message endures, for it is not possible to do everything by yourself, even though you may think you can—so you too will need to encourage and inspire others to join you on your journey.

Often someone's first startup begins with a single cofounder. So how do you choose the right cofounder? If you're currently in a business relationship with someone, you already know some of their best features;

is this someone who best completes you? Two technical cofounders can initiate a startup, but there will be a time where one of them will need to take on more of the nontechnical functions, including management, human resources, marketing, and, of extremely high importance, sales.

It's worth stating this again: as much as in the early days you won't believe it's necessary, and that it is not worth the expense, I would say that it is absolutely critical that you formally establish (through legal paperwork) the corporate structure, employment agreements detailing the structure of founders equity and a vesting schedule. Consider it as essential as a prenuptial agreement to a marriage. Many times people run out of steam in the first two years, leaving "dead equity" on the cap table.

Ian MacKinnon (founder and CTO of Later.com) has suggested that the "ideal" number of cofounders in a venture is $e$ – Euler's number. If you're unfamiliar with Euler's number, it's an irrational numerical constant of approximately 2.718. It, along with many potential cofounders you may encounter, is irrational. How many cofounders? Two or three are best.

You'll almost undoubtedly need to hire employees as you grow but recognize that you cannot expect that everyone will love your baby (the company) as much as you. In fact, if you can find competent employees who love your company even half as much as you do, that's a huge bonus. But don't count on it, and don't assume that will be the default.

To build on a point I've made previously: it is critical to assess and surmise a potential employee's motivation to join your company. Why would they specifically want to join your company? Despite what many say, an individual's salary component *is* important, but it is merely one facet of a more complicated Rubik's Cube. A new graduate might find your company more interesting than a larger competitor if they're motivated to avoid boredom. Someone in the middle of one's career who has spent time at larger enterprises might be tired of politicking and be looking for a different challenge. Alternatively, someone might be enticed by the possibility of pre-IPO options or equity within a startup. These motivations may also change; they're fluid, and you need to consider the broader macroeconomic environment. Startups may seem more appealing when tech giants like Apple and Google are laying off their employees.

When choosing potential employees, I suggest you start with the AAA principle: available, amicable, able—in that order. This was first suggested to me by my former colleague, Martin Loeffler, while we were working on a contract together. I'm not sure where it originated, but I have seen some reference to it when discussing the bedside manner of doctors. In any case, it applies across many industries.

**Available**: If they're not currently available (or will be as soon as you need them), nothing else matters. Along with being available, are they also in the same mindset: this is an ultramarathon, not a sprint. Not only will they need to commit to your project for the present time but for the foreseeable future. You'll need a commitment that they're not going to leave at the first sign of trouble. Also, if they're currently in a relationship, you'll need to make sure that their partner is also comfortable and committed to this joint endeavor. You'll all be in this together.

**Amicable**: Nobody likes an asshole, even a very competent and effective one. The startup grind will put stress on you and your team like you've likely never seen before. Ideally, you'll need to find someone who is generally amicable and can deal with stressful conditions. You might not know this in advance, so you might want to see if others within your network have had experiences with them. Feel free to reach out, offer to keep all conversations off the record, and if you do open up, do not disabuse their trust.

**Able**: If the candidate in mind is already available and amicable, only then should you consider their abilities. At this early stage, it is so important that the candidates have appropriate experience (or at least the flexibility to operate in the chaotic environment of a startup). I cannot emphasize this enough. A startup is no place for employees who just want to coast in their careers. It is not the final stop for someone queueing up to retire. You will need to carefully look at their personality and previous experience. If they're coming from a very stable corporate enterprise (such as enterprise sales or insurance technology departments), they will find the startup world to be shocking. I'm not saying that you shouldn't hire them, but if they've spent twenty years of their career in the same enterprise-sized environment, where many other departments (such as sales, marketing, and customer service) operated in their own silos, they might be decidedly uncomfortable when they're called upon to wear other hats—and I guarantee that in a startup, everyone will at some point need to wear multiple hats.

Now having said that, you need to assemble the very best team that you can afford. You need to surround yourself with people who want to see your endeavor succeed. I would add one caveat though: hire for impact, not for ego. Often people will ask, "How big is your company?" as though having hundreds of employees is better than a small lean team. Don't let your ego run amok when it comes to the size of your company.

### ABOUT FIRST HIRES

*The first few people we hired were co-op students from the University of Waterloo. Both my cofounder and I are UofW alumni and specifically had gone through the co-op program ourselves. There were (and still are) significant benefits to hiring co-op students. First, UofW computer science and engineering students have a reputation for being at the very top of the educational ladder. We were getting a chance to see exactly how well their education fit in the real world. Our first three co-op employees went on to work at Microsoft and Amazon after they graduated. A co-op term is generally four months in length, just enough time to complete several short sprints in execution. Four months is also enough time to get a strong sense of their work ethic, how well they could interact with the rest of the team, and most importantly, if they could mesh well with the firm's culture. If at the end of four months, either party could elect to return or go elsewhere—a frictionless model. In addition to getting access to young talent with newly acquired skills, when compared to full-time staff, co-op employees are relatively inexpensive. During their last work terms, their hourly rate approaches that of an entry-level developer position. In addition to their reasonable salary, there are often government programs that offer tax credits based on the wages paid to a student. Our first full-time staff member completed their final co-op terms with us.*

Just as there's such a thing as a minimally viable product, you should see if you can build a minimally viable team. Over-hiring can lead to immense problems, the least of all is burn rate or drain on cash flow. If you are lucky enough at some point, you may look at your well-optimized minimally viable team and think, "Wow, this is simply the perfect team."

Rest assured this will not last.

This "perfect team equilibrium" does not and cannot last. It is always in continual flux, as some people will depart, and new people will enter. You may find that a conflict arises from where one did not exist previously (as you will find when two or more coworkers were hired around the same time, yet only one is promoted). This "buddy-to-boss" scenario is endemic in technical startups. You will find that other disruptions to this elusive "perfect team" may include personal problems confronting staff, divorce, mental illness or substance abuse, stress at home, and even death. You will need to remain flexible and push forward whatever is thrown at you.

To maintain a sense of equilibrium, company culture is a huge and often unappreciated aspect of startup life. It will be difficult enough for you to find and hire people who are willing to buy into your dream. As the founder, you will find that both directly and indirectly; for better or for worse, you will set the tone for the corporate culture. Your best employees will embrace the culture you set and then, like a virus, help it spread. If you permit bullies to persist in the workplace, that too will permeate throughout the environment, both locally and outside the organization. If your go-to-market messaging emphasizes a sales process of ambulance-chasing salespeople or focusing unduly on the tactics of sowing fear, uncertainty, and doubt (FUD) among prospective clients, you will find it more difficult to find excellent employees committed to selling customers on your differentiated value proposition. You will need to set and maintain the tone throughout your journey. If you're a horse's ass, at some point, you will only attract other horse's asses to work with you—the market will understand what you are, and the crowding-out effect will keep others away. Now, perhaps you're working in a vertical where being a complete horse's ass is the norm or even desired. If that is the case, please feel free to ignore this paragraph.

As a leader, how can you help motivate, inspire, and act as a "guiding light' for your team? I would suggest that to start, you must demonstrate your ongoing commitment to your enterprise, that it is your primary focus and your constant care.

*Some companies pride themselves on their mission statement and/or publicly stated values declarations. Here is one as an example. (I have poached it from the back of one of their commemorative common share certificates.)*

## OUR VALUES

*Respect: We treat others as we would like to be treated ourselves. We do not tolerate abusive or disrespectful treatment. Ruthlessness, callousness, and arrogance don't belong here.*

*Integrity: We work with customers and prospects openly, honestly, and sincerely. When we say we will do something, we will do it; when we say we cannot or will not do something, then we won't do it.*

*Communication: We have an obligation to communicate. Here, we take the time to talk to one another and to listen. We believe that information is meant to move and that information moves people.*

*Excellence: We are satisfied with nothing less than the very best in everything we do. We will continue to raise the bar for everyone. The great fun here will be for all of us to discover just how good we can really be.*

*This is an example of a truly beautifully worded and carefully crafted value statement. I can't disagree with any of them.*

*However, this set of value statements belonged to the Enron Corporation, which had its CEO Jeffrey Skilling and CFO Andrew Fastow convicted of fraud and other offenses and sent to prison.*

Mission statements or publicly stated value declarations mean nothing if the entity itself is corrupt. My preference is for a "Commander's Intent" declaration.

Many years ago, at the very same Thayer leadership retreat mentioned earlier, we were asking how leadership could better communicate their future plans, intent, and attitude. Armed forces encounter specific structural difficulties with this, given the rigid hierarchies and massive numbers of people involved. They suggested the use of a commander's intent, the formal definition being as follows.

The "commander's intent" describes a desired end state. It is a concise statement of the purpose of the operation and must be understood two levels below the level of the issuing commander. It must clearly state the purpose of the missions. It is the single unifying focus for all subordinate elements. I prefer a somewhat more blended definition.

## ELDON SPRICKERHOFF'S COMMANDER'S INTENT/MISSION STATEMENT CROSS-PRODUCT FOR ESENTIRE

*"Work together to defend our clients by all reasonable means necessary, carefully planning for the maintainability and scalability of the measures and response taken, all the while ensuring the ongoing viability and growth of the business."*

*While I was working on my "commander's intent" statement, I had an idea of how to personalize it. During a quarterly all-hands meeting, I called up fellow employees across several different parts of the business, including sales, marketing, development, human resources, and finance.*

*In turn, I asked them each what their job was. The salesperson said, "I sell our cybersecurity services and offerings." The marketing person said, "I help to craft marketing messaging and programs to help sales." The developer said, "I write code." Our human resources representative said, "I work in HR, bringing new people into the company, managing any problems that might arise as we grow." Finally, the person in finance said, "I work in the finance department, accounts payable/receivable, managing costs and budgets."*

*I told them that their answers were all reasonable, but they were each essentially wrong.*

*A titter of laughter from the audience.*

*Each of their jobs was, in fact, to "defend our clients."*

*I didn't have someone from the Security Operations Center (SOC) up because they were the most directly connected to the pulse of the security landscape and were the front line in defending our clients. Nobody ever questions the SOC's direct value regarding defense.*

*But the others are perhaps a bit less obvious.*

*How do salespeople defend our clients? We can't defend our clients if we are insolvent. In order to stay solvent, we need to grow our revenue. Sales grow revenue, which helps us to stay solvent, and thereby allow us to continue to defend our clients.*

*How does marketing defend our clients? Marketing helps with the messaging and approach to support sales efforts (and so on).*

*How does tech development defend our clients? Developers work on solutions to better defend our clients but also to create new products for marketing to promote and salespeople to sell.*

*How does HR defend our clients? All the efforts made within the company are performed by our talented people. Our human resources department helps to manage staff within the entire company, helping to accomplish tasks and complete projects as needed.*

*Similarly, the finance department manages cash flow, collections, and future investments, directly responding to our solvency and efficacy and thereby defending our clients.*

*Each of these groups within the company, in their own way, working together, defends our clients.*

*Personalize the message.*

A significant part of your role as a founder is to provide a strong foundation for the company's growth. As the Chief Survival Officer, it is critical that you strike a balance between the raw truth and excessively sugar-coating reality. You will need to shoulder by yourself the vast majority of the stress during the most difficult times of the company's journey. I would recommend realistic yet tempered optimism as the tenor with which you provide company updates. All-hands meetings performed regularly can help to disseminate information. Gather questions beforehand (anonymously) and be prepared to answer them truthfully.

What else do you owe to your employees? I say that it is the duty of the founder to improve the socioeconomic status of your employees, especially at the beginning of your journey. Convincing others to join the company and build your dream may require a mass suspension of disbelief: infecting them with the very optimism you have.

Part of that charge to improve the socioeconomic status of your early-stage employees comes through granting equity where appropriate. There are many founders who jealously guard every single share of the company. Some take the express route of paying over market rates for employees in order to keep the equity portion to themselves. I am not of that mindset. When you finally get to the point where your company is worth enough for the equity to be important, there will be more than enough to share.

An Employee Stock Option Plan (ESOP) will probably be suggested by your investors after your Series A round is closed. It is of value to anticipate this and effect the mechanisms necessary to make this happen. Also, when the time is right (further into the future), it is of significant value to investigate the 409a valuation process. Recognize that if you are domiciled in the United States and started your company as a Limited Liability Corporation (LLC) you won't be able to issue shares or options, and as such you'll likely need to re-incorporate and repaper your startup as appropriate.

## ENTER HUMAN RESOURCES

As you continue to grow your company, you must build up and support your employees while they pursue their own goals on their career arc. Your company's success is what I consider the vector sum—adding together the components of each individual's success.

It is important that as you staff up your team appropriately, you follow the counsel of David Ricardo, the British economist who in 1817 coined the "Theory of Comparative Advantage" to explain why countries engage in international trade: in short, focus on that for which you are the best. This is particularly true of technical founders who find themselves needing to move into more executive or managerial roles but unwilling to give up the technical work. If this statement resonates with you, you will need to let it go. When you move from technical lead to a more managerial role, you will need to give your more junior staff the latitude to learn (and perhaps fail, as appropriate). I guarantee that none of them will perform a task in the same manner as you believe you would. There's a song lyric refrain, the original source for which is unknown, which states, "*The hardest part of love is letting go.*" And there's a lot of truth in that cheesy lyric.

You will need to learn different skills as you grow. Just like your startup is your "baby" and is maturing, so you are, too. You'll find that you'll need to change your perspective so that it is less focused on management and more on leadership. It is a subtle difference, a subtlety you'll learn to appreciate more and more as you grow.

In this vein, and I cannot emphasize this enough, hire slowly, fire quickly. I have never had to terminate someone's employment and later thought,

"I should have let them go later." The first time that you terminate someone is among the most nerve-wracking and stressful positions you will find yourself in, mostly because it is personal. But pay heed: rip the bandage off. Ultimately, you need to do what is best for the company and its survival. One bad fish can kill the entire tank, and at the beginning of your journey, your tank is particularly susceptible to even the smallest negative changes in climate. It is best for both of you to close this particular shared chapter at the earliest appropriate moment.

*We had a specific team leader (hired through an acquisition) who should not have been placed in that position. While on paper they had the appropriate experience and credentials, their interpersonal skills were not their forte and nowhere near what was required. This was made abundantly clear when, after a few months of working with them, every member of that seven-person team resigned within 10 days of each other.*

*The team lead was sure that each departing team member had excellent (and different) reasons for leaving including "more money," "better opportunity," "spend more time with their family," and "had been here long enough." Within their exit interviews, none of the departing team members mentioned the toxic relationship with their team lead (careful not to burn bridges), but it was evident and widely discussed outside the 9–5 workday.*

*When seven employees leave in a cluster, it is most likely that there is a core common reason. It is said that people don't leave companies; they leave poor management. To wit, I repeat: fire quickly, especially if the core issue cannot be mitigated or resolved and may not even be acknowledged by the supervisor.*

In my role as a mentor, I've seen a tendency for startups to hire too many people too quickly (especially after they've raised a round of capital). People in general are expensive, and very good people are very expensive. Especially at the beginning, hire slowly, hire generalists who offer some overlap (in case of attrition), and hire in rhythm to your sales plan and revenue targets. In the early days, you might discover that some remarkably competent employees are capable of wearing multiple hats. This can be valuable, but you must take care: if you load up on people with multiple responsibilities, you may be enabling a single point of failure. If that person chooses to give their two weeks' notice, you will likely scramble to reallocate their responsibilities.

If you find yourself in a dire cash-burn situation, you may be forced to lay off people, and that obviously injects a broad negative effect across the firm. If you need to lay off your "least-essential" employees, you can be sure that your "most-essential' employees will be circulating their resumes.

## EXITING THE TOXIC EMPLOYEE

The late, great chef Anthony Bourdain in his book *Kitchen Confidential (Adventures in the Culinary Underbelly)*, written in 2000, has a chapter called "Department of Human Resources," where he discusses the quandary of a high-performing though difficult employee of one of his former protégés. This particular cook had been "showing up late, not showing up, getting high at work, behaving insolently, and fomenting dissent among his co-workers." Bourdain adds context: "Convinced that the whole kitchen revolved around his station, his mood swings and his toil, he felt free to become a raving, snarling, angry lunatic—a dangerously loose cannon rolling around on deck, just daring his chef and his co-workers to press the wrong button."

With any luck, you'll never have to deal with such a difficult employee. However, given a long enough tenure, you will undoubtedly come across someone who believes they have an outsized role in the organization and aren't being given appropriate compensation or appreciation for their efforts. They might start gossiping or spreading dissent among their fellow employees.

This is a particularly tough situation, especially during the early days of your startup, where the chain is only as strong as its weakest link. No matter how talented this employee is, how critical they are to the operation, or how much of a "rock star" they may appear, they can break the chain. You cannot tolerate the stress fracture for long.

An infected wound can fester. A cancer can metastasize and kill the patient.

It's unlikely, in my experience, that they will improve. You might not yet have a formal human resources employee in your organization, so you will likely need to tread carefully. You need to terminate them or, rather, "free them from the bondage of their employment."

It's better to rip the Band-Aid off but with the proper supports in place.

Ensure that you have sufficient documentation detailing the various misdeeds of the employee (with dates and times listed). Contact a lawyer well versed in employment law to determine what the best course of action should be—this may widely differ depending on the domicile of the employee. If you have an HR professional within your network, it can be helpful to discuss with them (under confidentiality) what options you might have.

Prepare to have the soon-to-be-sacked employee's login and other credentials locked out and reset before the formal termination is completed. This might be problematic (especially if they're a technical resource whose job includes maintaining credentials and data security), so be sure you have more than one person who can swiftly handle these duties.

When you need to sit down with the employee to terminate, do not meet alone. You should expect that the employee in question may lash out, verbally or even physically. Do not give reasoning behind the decision; you don't want your words to come back to bite you. Inform them that their employment is terminated; they will need to sign a release acknowledging that, and they will shortly be given a package regarding the terms of their release (including severance pay, vacation days accrued, status of vested options, and possibly access to an employment professional to help them find their next position). It is critical that they are given time to review the terms of their severance, so they aren't able to claim that they were made to sign under duress.

You should anticipate that it's unlikely that they'll accept the first offer that you make, so you should preplan some wiggle room for them to negotiate. For example, if they are legally able to receive two weeks of severance, offer them three weeks of severance (giving them more than is legally required) but with the anticipation that they will reply with four weeks (which you will concede).

Ultimately, you want this headache off your plate quickly so that you can move forward mending the damage left behind.

*At one of my previous employers, a new management team came in, and as a result, there was a broad request (more like a demand) made of all employees to update and submit their resumes. It was self-evident that the company would be restructured in some manner. As a result, productivity stalled while everyone was paid to update their resumes. After the resumes were gathered and assessed, management declared that there would be some restructuring and terminations forthcoming. In two weeks' time, they would be made public. Why they chose to wait two weeks to make the final announcement is beyond me. Unsurprisingly, two eventual outcomes resulted from this declaration. First, project progress stalled throughout the company. Second, almost everyone who had valuable skills put their newly updated resumes out into the market. When the two-week period ended, there were a dozen employees who were terminated. No one was surprised that specific employees were terminated—they were not "top performers" (and you know that in a small enough organization, everyone in their hearts knows the people who aren't the top-level talent). However, in the following two months, there was a second exodus of talented people who had received job offers with better compensation. The company never quite bounced back from this exodus. Disclosure: I was one of the employees in the second group.*

Judiciously hire the best and most appropriate people you can afford for where you currently are and where you plan to be in the near future. It is perhaps not immediately obvious, but at each stage of your company, there will be people better suited for the available positions. In a subsequent chapter (relating to sales), I will give a specific description of a senior enterprise-level salesperson from a publicly traded company who was hired into a startup with less-than-stellar results.

I have noted that every time you double your staff headcount, you face an entirely new set of growing pains that you will need to address. While this might include dealing with "technical debt" appropriate to scaling— technical debt refers to the costs of future reconfigurations required after having implemented an easy but limited solution instead of a better approach that could take more time—I have found that most of the time the hard issues relate to people. You will find that there are few people who are comfortable at the very beginning of a startup all the way through to its blossoming into a large formal enterprise. This may include you. It is the rare founder who can pivot and remain both relevant and inspiring as the company grows and scales.

As I've said earlier, employee communication is critical. You will soon recognize that not everyone communicates in the same manner. As the founder, it is essential that you choose your words carefully but also that you recognize that others may have difficulty communicating with you in the way that you need to understand and appreciate their concerns. I recommend getting ahead of potential issues, using radical candor with an empathic manner. Isolate concerns, surface them readily, examine roadblocks, and dissect troublesome behavior early and in a frank and transparent manner. That might mean as simple a question to one of your employees as "What's going on, Frank?"

> One fellow team member in charge of the operations center would frequently knock on my door and say: "We have a problem!" Instantly, my adrenaline would start pumping, and he would have my complete attention, even to the detriment of whatever else I was working on. Much more often than not, the problem to which he was bringing to my attention was of a low priority, say two out of ten. I mulled over this inconsistency until I was able to later make sense of it.
>
> He was both an engineer and a pilot. I am neither!
>
> Pilots are trained to follow strict processes and checklists. Safety is paramount, and even small problems can lead to larger issues. The margin of error in the air is considerably smaller than for a business on the ground. When I took his personal point of view into consideration, my heart raced considerably less the next time he came to my office.

As an aside to running the business, make sure you get an excellent lawyer, an accountant, and a bookkeeper with whom your excellent accountant can work. You don't necessarily need to go to a white-shoe law firm or a top-tier accounting firm, but find people with experience with startups who can help you make the best decisions regarding registering your business, drafting contracts, bookkeeping, and so on. Nothing is more expensive than a cheap lawyer or accountant, or one who is unfamiliar with your stage of company, domicile, and geography of clients. You don't want to do this yourself. From the very beginning, document everything, especially when establishing equity for cofounders. It can be very difficult to untangle equity ownership positions if the relationship starts to unravel.

You should not expect that your bookkeeper and accountant will be solely responsible to raise an alarm when cash flow is at a critical point. As the founder, you need to regularly keep a watchful eye, at least on a monthly basis, to keep track of cash flow and prepare to manage difficulties with some foresight (suggesting a few quarters' ahead doesn't seem unreasonable). I'm willing to bet that a significant number of startups fail due to cash flow issues (sometimes arising from failures in consistent billing practices or from poor follow-up on collecting amounts unpaid for work completed). (One study by *CB Insights* mentioned in a 2023 article on Metics.io noted that 82 percent of startups fail due to cash flow problems.) And on this point, reserve tax revenues and ensure that tax outlays and payments are made on time.

If you forget about the importance of cash flow to your startup's survival, you may quickly discover to your surprise that you no longer have a business.

## FLASH AND CASH FLOW

*There will be a tendency at the beginning to be very flashy about your new company. This could include a fancy office space, embroidered swag, huge conference booths, or other similarly expensive distractions. From the very start, I recommend that you be mindfully frugal with your spending. Every dollar should scream out when you spend it.*

*When we started eSentire (in the days before inexpensive long-distance phone calls, Skype, Zoom, Microsoft Teams, or other remote connectivity tooling), we used phone cards to reduce our costs. If we needed to fly into Manhattan for meetings, we would drive to Buffalo International Airport and fly on the newly established JetBlue Airways (it was often one-tenth the price of a direct flight from Toronto Pearson International Airport to JFK), and take the AirTrain to the Long Island Rail Road into Penn Station. We would share rooms while staying in some of the cheapest hotels you could imagine, and we exclusively used public transit unless there was no other option. There were times (like during New York Fashion Week) that we could not even afford the cheapest hotel in the city; we would take the first flight out in the morning, have a solid day's worth of meetings, and then sprint back to the airport for the last flight of the day.*

*Especially at the beginning, make calculated and prudent decisions regarding how money is spent. There is value in an "abundance mindset," but the survival of your startup can't solely be manifested into existence with an inspirational dreamscape alone. Don't run out of money before you get to your first destination. There will be a time for greater extravagance (let the investment bankers pay for that at the closing dinner after a big deal gets completed).*

You're assembling your team; it is now time to review the methods to which you will bring your offering to market. We need to assess your go-to-market (GTM) strategies. It is unlikely that you'll be able to succeed without convincing others to join your team. At the earliest stages, you will need to be especially careful with your hiring choices. One weak link rusts the chain and snaps it. You are responsible for establishing and maintaining the culture for the company. Your employees depend on you to set the tone and provide guidance and direction to maintain its health and vitality.

# CHAPTER 8

# Go-to-Market Preparation

A FIRST-TIME FOUNDER MIGHT NOT even have thought about a go-to-market strategy. I know I hadn't. Without a thorough evaluation of the product offering and potential market approaches, the likelihood of success is significantly diminished.

*I'm going to share certain pieces of one specific early heartbreak and how it can help build a framework for a go-to-market strategy.*

*There is a nonprofit innovation group called the Canadian Network for Advancement Research Industry Education (known as CANARIE) that supports a variety of initiatives to help Canadian organizations develop innovative applications and technologies. CANARIE serves as Canada's National Research and Education Network (NREN), connecting the country's researchers, educators, and innovators to each other and to global data, technology, and partners. The organization collaborates with provincial and territorial partners to form the NREN, and it's a key player in strengthening the security of Canada's research and education sector through cybersecurity initiatives. In mid-2002, CANARIE had opened some tenders for grant proposals, so we applied for funding (via an EOI, short for an "Expression of Interest") for a managed information security services offering. In January of the following year, we received the following response:*

*"We thought that your EOI was well done and that your proposal is very interesting in many respects. However, our position was to not conduct a further review of your proposal."*

*Ouch.*

*This was a swift blow to the solar plexus.*

*Upon careful review, however, the grant reviewers were wholly correct in their reasoning to reject our EOI. Let me dig a little deeper for you:*

**Target Market and MVP**: *"As presented your offering is very generic and is targeted at a very broad market, making it difficult to evaluate its real potential for success." Indeed, we hadn't yet identified our minimally viable product (MVP).*

**Validation from Intended Market**: *"We are very unlikely to support a proposal that cannot demonstrate that the market has been well qualified for your solution." We had not yet identified anything as simple as a total addressable market (TAM) or sales Addressable Market (SAM).*

**Go-to-market Approach**: *"We would need to have a better understanding of your penetration strategies and a realistic mapping of your required marketing costs." We had not identified any facets of a reasonable go-to-market approach, including costs associated with that approach.*

*__Revenue Model__: "A clearer picture in terms of the underlying revenue assumptions would be needed to understand and assess the effort and cost that would be required to reach the level of revenue projected." We had not quantified effort, customer acquisition costs, or revenue projections.*

*They closed with a final missive: "We hope that these comments will be of value to you . . . and wish you all the best in your future plans."*

*I called this our first "Dear John" letter. It was heartbreaking. It was devastating. It also hit a bullseye in its accuracy.*

At the time we were still in the startup reverie of having built a better mousetrap without taking into consideration what the market wanted and how to present it to the market. Of course, at the time we didn't have either the resources or talent to correct or execute CANARIE's observations. Eventually, we did manage to mature and address these glaring gaps, but at the same time, this was a depressing bucket of ice-cold water dumped on us.

I want to use the key points from the CANARIE "Dear John" letter as a framework for the next few chapters.

The letter was a big reveal: You will need to (at least in broad strokes) sketch out what your offering (service or product) is, what will be the most attractive market for you to chase, how you'll reach out to clients, and what will be your plan to grow revenue.

# CHAPTER 9

# MVP, One Acronym That Really Matters

S O MANY TECH STARTUPS begin with what I would consider a graduation "capstone" or "science fair project"—an interesting idea, hypothesis, or feature that might have some broader application outside of a lab or academia. It may not actually be enough to form a company, but there's undoubtedly *something* there. The leap from an interesting idea or "alpha offering" to a standalone offering worthy of investment or use in the real world may be considered your minimally viable product (MVP). A well-defined MVP is critical for several reasons.

It is important to shepherd your offering into the real world; the feedback that you get on your MVP is critical to your success going forward. An MVP allows you to test market demand and to see if there is a genuine appetite for it in the market; in other words, does it offer features that potential users need? No amount of third-party market research and analysis will give you the amount of valuable feedback once your first MVP gets released. This feedback should include ease of use, perceived value, pricing and monetization, competitive advantage against competitors, and, ultimately, the feedback will help to determine, quantify, and forecast appetite in the market—from both a customer and investor perspective.

When honing your MVP it is critically important to frequently communicate and listen to customers, prospects, and design partners to identify which components solve the most pain for them. Early in the process, when you are discussing features you need to determine how important this solution would be to solve their pain points. Questions you need to ask should include:

- Is this an actual problem or is this merely an existential problem for you?
- Is it a big problem for you, and is it growing as time passes?
- Is there another solution that currently exists to solve this problem?
- Could this solution save you money?
- How much would you pay for this solution? What would it take for you to pay for this solution?

These questions should help to identify which features to include in your MVP, and which might need to be put on a roadmap for future development.

Once you "break the seal" with an MVP, you're then free to iterate and gradually refine and improve the MVP. Without an MVP, it is difficult to determine pricing, customer interest, and demand, and whether your business actually has any chance at survival.

## INSPIRATION FOR AN MVP

*Inspiration for new or adjacent offerings may come from the most unexpected places at the most unexpected times.*

*Despite having taken many advanced courses in computer science, I have never been a great programmer or developer. However, I have a certain dexterity in ideation and in making connections between disparate modules or components. The stories that follow may help make sense of what I mean.*

*Once I had been asked by the Credit Suisse Prime Brokerage unit to speak at a panel during its day-long conference for hedge fund chief technology officers. There were two cybersecurity panels in the morning; I was scheduled to sit on the second one. While sitting in the audience for the first panel, I was listening to the panelists and noted that one said something surprising and alarming: "There are hundreds of attacks on hedge funds every day, and nobody has any idea of what they look like." With a jolt, I sat up straight in abrupt disbelief. Explaining threat attacks and how to spot them was our precise mandate at eSentire. While the speaker kept talking, I had an idea crystalize in my mind. Up until that point, if we saw some inappropriate behavior at a single client, we would enable the specific "deny list" at that particular client to stop that attack (generally it was from an external attacker). The small moment of inspiration I had in that moment was to extend that capability, which would protect that single client under the ambit of a broader umbrella of cover, to thereby protect all clients. I started sketching out what that could possibly look like—literally on a napkin in front of me on the table. I brought it back to the office the next day. Within two weeks we had a working, functional model of our global IP address deny capability. To this day, the asset manager protect (AMP) functionality is used within eSentire (even keeping the name that I had originally chosen for it). It has helped to defend against hundreds of millions of inbound attacks against our client base.*

*A second inspirational moment: at eSentire we had been building out deep packet inspection (DPI) capabilities with the Ragel language and extensible framework created by Dr. Adrian Thurston, one of our incredibly capable early employees. DPI permitted us to quickly analyze network traffic and make decisions based on what was interpreted. Separate modules could quickly identify details such as domain names, components within URLs, and help stitch together separate packets to identify "executables" (or more commonly: "programs"). On March 25, 2009, I was attending the monthly Toronto Area Security Klatch (TASK) event. A fellow startup entrepreneur, Dave Millier, was speaking about the capabilities of whitelisting activity—a form of endpoint security that helps organizations increase their cybersecurity by only allowing approved and trusted applications to run while blocking all others. As I was listening to his talk, I suddenly felt a moment of inspiration strike. We had a DPI module that could recognize domains and URL structures, another DPI module that could identify executables being downloaded, some network functionality that could inject interlaced bidirectional reset (RST) packets into a network traffic stream, and I knew we could force a browser to reload a requested webpage. If we could add a whitelisting component, to draw from a list of "domains from which it is acceptable to download executables," we could prevent drive-by downloads of malicious executables. We had months' worth of data to build that domain list across all clients. The next morning I sketched out on a whiteboard this idea; within a week, we had a working model of what I ultimately called "the EXEcutioner." We quickly rolled out the functionality across our client base and almost immediately prevented thousands of drive-by downloads, without the need for alerting clients or installing updates. Previously, our clients would need to completely rebuild their endpoint systems; this was no longer the case.*

*These two specific inspirational moments led to iterative product offerings that were so helpful and beneficial to our client base that they helped eSentire become one of the stickiest cybersecurity companies in the world: that meant that our clients considered our offerings "must-haves," not "nice-to-haves." Even better: this helped to reduce the workload of the security operations centers by proactively defending against attacks that likely would have succeeded and demanded hands-on attention. Truly a win-win.*

*You don't know when or where inspiration will hit you. If I had not attended either (or both) of the Credit Suisse CTO forum or TASK events, I might not have been exposed to the triggers that ultimately helped me formulate the improved service offerings that have become core to the business today. Be open to new perspectives and think about how this new information could be incorporated into your current product offering as an improvement to benefit your customer base.*

*Even one truly inspirational development can dramatically change your startup's trajectory for the better and for years to come. Some facets of inspiration have an extremely long tail. When they strike you, be receptive to investigating them.*

Through the earliest days of your MVP, you might have the opportunity to find your "True Believer" clients—those customers who will become your bread-and-butter clients. These are the individuals who are so excited in your offering that they are thrilled for you to succeed. If you're lucky, they will be so invested in your success that they will stake their reputation and career on it. If this is the case, you must ensure that you are as invested in their career as they are in the success of your endeavor.

Consider their perspective: they're in a good place with their workplace, and a virtually unknown little startup wants you to spend the time, energy, and effort to see if this new and/or unproven solution is right for you. If it fails, it is a stain on their record. Nobody wants the residue of failure on them from their full-time job. Recognize their motivation and work to help them succeed.

You may not yet know precisely how or where your offering will be used in the hands of your customers. As the sci-fi writer William Gibson has said: "The street finds its own use for things." It is important that you listen to your customers—particularly those early adopter types who seem to be better attuned to the future than others. They may have particularly insightful ideas that you have not yet considered.

*From the very beginning of eSentire, we were interested in creating a managed security services offering but found it difficult to find customers who were immediately willing to commit to that. Either they didn't see the value of an ongoing managed service, didn't see there was a problem that needed to be solved, couldn't find the budget due to other priorities, or simply didn't trust us. We were committed to focusing on information security—we could have gone down the road of building out infrastructure for clients but that was already a fairly saturated market, and doing so would have muddied our MVP focus and company vision. We had made the commitment from the very beginning that we were to solely be an information security company—that was that, and there was to be no deviation.*

*To survive, we started to focus on vulnerability assessments for consulting revenue. Vulnerability scanning was considered a necessary dimension to ongoing due diligence. At the time, the vast majority of vulnerability assessments that were pitched to clients and performed by practitioners in the market were rather simplistic: scan the external network, this network consisting of just those systems that were visible from the broad internet perspective. Further complicating the definition of vulnerability assessments were that some practitioners would confuse clients by wrongly calling them "penetration tests" though no actual penetration testing work would be achieved. This was still the easiest and most "low hanging fruit" of consulting—you could automate it to perform the scans and print out a thick report of potential threat attacks that could educate clients and thereafter entice them into buying additional services.*

*We chose to extend the scope of vulnerability assessments; at the time, it was a bold and radical move. We would perform a scan of the external infrastructure (like everyone else did), but we would also scan the internal infrastructure and install a network sensor onsite to capture and analyze network traffic (looking for indicators of concern and network compromise). We would perform the vulnerability scans during off-peak hours and analyze the traffic that occurred during regular business hours.*

*There were several virtuous outcomes that came from our approach.*

1. *We "raised the bar" for what was expected from others when a vulnerability scan was needed. The external-facing report was used for due diligence and compliance perspectives, while the internal-facing report was used by the client alone to improve their cybersecurity stance.*

2. *We were able to find more valuable information from the network traffic than from the scanning alone. Information gained from active traffic visibility was of far greater value than that derived from more passive scanning queries.*

3. *If we saw something unusual from the network traffic, we could perform a deeper analysis and immediately report it to the client. Whereas the clients would be comfortable with receiving vulnerability scanning results in a week's time (if there was nothing critical detected), reports of attacks happening at the very moment provided a level of visibility*

*and insight not previously encountered in the market. The client could then take immediate action to remedy the problem detected.*

4. *This activity engendered trust in our process, our people, our technology, and our company.*

5. *Once the vulnerability assessment engagement was completed, with the report submitted and the closing meeting with a presentation finished, the client didn't want to remove the network sensor. Its value had been demonstrated to them, and they didn't want to lose that.*

6. *Through this process, we were able to build out the beginnings of a managed services offering, winning us what we needed: recurring revenues.*

7. *We gained an excellent reputation for doing what others weren't doing and were able to describe to other potential clients what we had found in their peers' environments.*

8. *Our happiest clients would become active and voluble references for us. They wanted us to succeed and continue helping defend them.*

*We also changed our own mindset through this process. Instead of looking at a vulnerability assessment as a single work item or project, we approached it as though the client would definitely want to keep the network sensor in place, so we wouldn't assume that we would retrieve it at the end of the engagement. This subtle mind shift helped to frame the process and focus on the end goal of growing new revenues.*

*By redefining what clients should expect from a "standard vulnerability assessment," we were able to differentiate ourselves against the rest of the market and change what could have been a low-margin loss leader project to a healthy sales pipeline to a more valuable and "sticky" managed services offering.*

In the MVP ideation process you need to determine what is the smallest (e.g., atomic) offering that you can sell at a reasonable profit margin with a minimum of friction and for which there is demand in the market? What problem does it solve? How does it differ from what else is available in the market? Thanks to your insight, can you propose some variation that others have not yet seen?

Define and package this small yet powerful bundle; market and sell it like hotcakes. Once you find some success in a small yet significant offering, you can extend or pivot from there to grow further.

# CHAPTER 10

# Your Ideal Customer

**H**AVE YOU IDENTIFIED TO whom you will be selling your offering? Who is your ideal customer? How do you find your ideal customer and convert them into your "True Believers" or "Johnny Appleseeds," spreading the word about the great work you do?

*As I've detailed, our first dozen sales at eSentire were within the hedge fund/ alternative investment advisor vertical—to companies in the "buy-side" of finance, the segment of the financial market consisting of investing institutions that purchase investment securities. I remember that we had a meeting where we had an inbound sales invitation from a potential customer who was far outside the client vertical with which we had the most comfort (it was a huge publicly traded mining company). In this meeting, there was considerable discussion around the table as to whether we should stray outside of our original client base vertical.*

*I had a moment of clarity and suggested the following characteristics of our best clients:*

1. *They needed to be willing and able to pay us.*
2. *They had data that was important and valuable.*
3. *They recognized that they had a need for improved information security capabilities (capabilities commonly detailed as "confidentiality, integrity, and availability").*
4. *They had multiple offices (possibly in very different jurisdictions or geographies) without sufficient visibility into their security stance.*
5. *They had regulatory concerns regarding their operations and data.*

*These characteristics did not pigeonhole us into only servicing financial customers. And we did indeed go on to bring the company from within the mining vertical onboard as a client. This was the first of many clients to stretch us beyond our initial pocket of customers within the buy-side financial vertical.*

What are the characteristics of *your* perfect client? If you can't clearly define this, you'll waste your time thrashing around, disappointed by the lack of traction. While you might want to sell your product to every single person in the world, it is not possible—and in any case, you'll need to identify who are the ideal earliest candidates.

The best source for sourcing potential clients starts within your contacts. Your own network (including previous employers and fellow former employees) must be the first group to which you introduce your offering. Don't be shy. Hopefully, you will have kept in touch with them on a regular basis while you've been grinding away and improving upon your startup. Keep in mind that no one wants to be perceived simply as a commodity, a source from which you continually extract value without providing any progress updates or reciprocation in return. With any luck, they will be able to offer you advice and/or referrals if there's anyone within their network who might find your solution interesting. In defining your ideal client, you'll stop yourself from wasting time chasing clients in verticals where you have less likelihood of success.

Your first ideal client (especially if you're looking for design partners) will fall within the Venn diagram of three categories:

1. They have a problem (or pain point) that they can describe.
2. They believe that you have (or can build) a solution to solve that problem and/or soothe that pain.
3. They're able to contribute some of their budget to help you solve the problem and ease their pain.

Advice from others who aren't able to contribute funding to match (e.g. "put their money where their mouth is") is suboptimal when compared to the ideal situation.

## CHAPTER 11

# The Advisory Board (versus the Board of Directors)

A N ADVISORY BOARD SHOULD comprise individuals with direct or related experience in your field but not in a competitive capacity. They should be able to provide actionable advice on how to achieve success. You will undoubtedly need to reach throughout your network to find individuals who can meet on a regular basis (at least once a quarter) to help boost your company's growth. Ideally, you will want to assemble a team of advisors with different yet complementary core competencies: strategy, finance, fund-raising, management, and sales growth. Typically, you will grant a small percentage of your equity to these advisors, depending on how much time and effort they can commit and will expend and what specific benefits you expect them to bring to your company.

Not everyone whom you invite to be on your advisory board will accept. You are asking that potential advisory board member to commit to your risky endeavor and, in turn, to put their own reputation on the line. They may decline for many different reasons, including the fact that they might not find your offering sufficiently interesting or even viable or within their scope of expertise. It's also possible they're not willing or able to make the time commitment necessary.

It is critical that you nominate a lead, an advisory board chair. The chair will work with your internal team to curate content, guide discussion flow, and moderate any issues that may arise during their time on the advisory board.

An adjacent approach (later in your startup journey) is that of a customer advisory board (CAB), with members drawn from a subset of your "most trusted" customer base. During a customer advisory board meeting, you should be able to solicit feedback for upcoming offerings, work through any customer feedback concerns, and, more broadly, give the CAB a window into your product and strategic roadmap to enable them to help you chart out your firm's future.

Both an advisory board and a customer advisory board are less formal creatures than a board of directors because they have no governance authority or statutory responsibilities. Advisory boards can meet less frequently and be consulted on an ad hoc basis as required. The approval of strategy and assessment of risks are subjects properly reserved for the main board. An advisory board can support the board by providing expert insight or contacts, but it must be clear where ultimate decision-making authority and collective responsibility lie—with the board of directors, to whom the CEO is accountable.

Regarding building a formal board of directors: there's little value in creating a board of directors before you've raised substantial capital (for example, in a Series A round). At that point, you should assume that any significant investor will demand a seat on the board as a condition of their investment. It is valuable to keep a few specific people in mind (particularly when you need to find an independent board member), but it's not necessary to build up a formal board of directors at the earliest stages; focus on surviving and growing your company for now. If an early-stage investor (pre-seed or seed) demands a seat on a (possibly nonexistent) board, you should strongly reconsider taking their investment.

## FINDING THE RIGHT
## (OR WRONG) ADVISORS

There will be people who offer their advisory services to you—beware. As wonderful as the offer might be, recognize that they're selling themselves to you, and as such their intentions might not be particularly altruistic. How can you find the most effective advisors?

First, I've already discussed the AAA principle in an earlier chapter when discussing early hires. Let's start there: go back and reread it.

Second, consider their experience; is it recent enough to be of value to you as you grow? If they've been "off the market" for any considerable amount of time, it's unlikely that they have a sense as to your current challenges and specifics regarding how to resolve them.

Third, is their experience in the market beneficial to your current endeavor? If not exact, is it at least adjacent? For example, you wouldn't expect someone with experience in manufacturing to necessarily be able to give guidance regarding the sales mechanisms of software-as-a-service (SaaS).

Fourth, do they bring complementary strengths to your existing advisory board? Some overlap in skillset is valuable, but you should be looking for breadth.

Fifth, do they have a current network into which they can introduce you and your service offering? If they commit to doing so, then this proves that they believe in you and are committed to your success.

Be sure to perform a background check, seeking both formal and informal (off-the-record) checks from people within your network to ensure whether there will be a match. It's always a good idea to go through your own network and see if there are business operators who can serve as reference checks on your potential advisors and are able to describe their own experiences while working with them—especially if they worked together through challenging times. Be comfortable asking the difficult questions. Do not settle for a mediocre advisor. You may learn that after several months their advice is not worth it so structure their equity around milestones, include both an earn-out and a cliff.

Recognize that following the advice of an advisor is what I refer to as a "ham and eggs" problem. While the eggs come from a chicken and the ham comes from a pig, for one, it's a donation, and for the other it's a commitment. You should not expect that any advisor will fly in to magically save you and your business. As in any potentially valuable resource, there are few very good advisors who are worth the equity. You might very well find that the best advice comes from people who are willing to invest some of their own money in your business.

The right mentors and advisors can help you succeed by expanding your network, identifying opportunities, and offering guidance on your ideas and direction.

# CHAPTER 12

# Founder-Led Sales

ENERALLY, AS A FIRST-TIME tech founder, you might not have yet realized how important the sales function is. As I've stated earlier, "even though you might build the best mousetrap ever, the world will not beat its way to your door." You're going to need someone selling.

At the very beginning, that likely means you or one of your cofounders. If your entire staff is fully technical and not particularly of the sales mindset, *congratulations*: it is you, you're IT, unless you can outsource it (and you probably shouldn't want to outsource it yet).

You will be wearing multiple hats at the beginning of your journey as the Chief Survival Officer, but sales are among the most important ones.

Plenty of technical founders hate the sales process, especially if your personality tends toward introversion. Perhaps you've had bad experiences with salespeople in the past. Perhaps you believe they're all some variant of a "used car salesman" or "professional liars" or that they're "getting paid to take people out to lunch after a golf game." Those are unfair generalizations.

If you're uncomfortable with the prospect of selling, if you truly detest it, you better learn to suck it up. Unless you're going to outsource sales to a cofounder, there's no way to succeed without some initial effort at getting your offering out to the public. Even the most viral of applications had an early struggle period before achieving notability. As the Chief Survival Officer, you will need to spend some portion of your time in a sales capacity, even if you're not formally selling to potential clients. Get used to it. Founder authenticity is a superpower, and if you're going up against larger, better-known, and better-financed competition, you're going to need everything you've got.

Take some solace in the fact that practically every single successful tech company started in this manner: acquiring customers through founder-led sales. Though you may feel almost physical pain or even revulsion at the sales process, you need to admit that at this specific point in time, there is no one else who can sell the vision and your offering better than you can. No one believes in the offering as much as you, and no one else can demonstrate the same passion and commitment you have to its success. If your endeavor is going to succeed, you as the Chief Survival Officer are going to need to be the Chief Revenue Officer as well.

Using your own definition of "ideal customers" referred to earlier in this book as your guide, compile a list of contacts (also known as unqualified prospects). In the early days, you will need to rely on your own network, coupled with soft introductions from your advisors.

Work on your thirty-second elevator pitch; explain in plain language (without technical jargon) what you do. Test it with friends and other founders before you go out into the world. On an ongoing basis, compile a list of client objections you can think of (or you've heard). Over time, you may want to compile a list of answers to those objections, too.

When you have created the list and with any luck booked a sales meeting with these unqualified prospects, devote significant time to prepare for it! Ahead of time, research the backgrounds of the company and the attendees. Be respectful and grateful to any advisors who extended their good name and reputation to land you the meeting. Tailor your presentation to your audience, and be respectful of their time and their knowledge.

If possible, meet in person. Remote meetings have been made somewhat of a default post-COVID-19, but I'm of the belief that demonstrating your respect for a prospect requires of you the effort to meet with them on their home turf. If you're using a presentation (like PowerPoint), keep it succinct; also make sure you have multiple physical printouts available in case of technical failure. Describe the problem you're solving with specifics as to how you address and solve real-world problems. Most importantly, ask for their feedback and gauge their interest. Make notes. I have found that your chances for success improve when you let the prospect themselves describe their pain points.

If there are several people in attendance, watch for their subtle body language to determine seniority, attentiveness, and technical role-playing. Try and ascertain product-market fit: do not be afraid to ask if this is something they're interested in and if it is a problem with which they're currently struggling. If it is a pain point, determine if it is a priority. If the problem you solve isn't a high priority, you should try to determine if there is an alternative or adjacent use of your offering that could address one of their highest priorities. This information can help you adjust your MVP.

At the end of the first introductory meeting, don't be afraid to make the ask: specifically, identify action items (on both sides, if appropriate) and book the next meeting into the calendar. If there's been interest shown, the unqualified prospect turns into a qualified prospect and keeps that sales momentum going.

As you proceed in this fashion, make it very easy for the prospect to see how they can benefit from your offering. For example, build a path to follow along the lines of "This is how some of our other clients have successfully rolled out our solution in a pilot program." Ideally, you should try to help build an internal business case for them.

Pricing is exceedingly tricky. I would suggest asking your trusted advisors for their opinions. The first few paying customers are critical, and you're better off heavily discounting from the list price in order to gain "logos," a sales term for earned clients. Seasoned salespeople will ask something along the lines of "We want your business and you've shown this could be valuable to you. What would our solution be worth to your business if we were to solve this problem for you?" Personalize the ask.

Whatever your offering, don't give it away for free. Don't offer to give it away for free. When you give anything away for free, it is rarely seen as something of value. I despise leaving any money on the table. However, there is value in offering a time-limited trial version if the cost of doing so is minimal. Be sure to track the usage of the "freemium" or demonstration model and take time to see what components they use most. Fold this information into the next version of your product (or tweak the current MVP). If you have found that the user of your "freemium" model has opted out of email updates (or has put themselves on the "do not contact" list), I would recommend that you pause their use of the offering. You're not the reincarnation of Mother Teresa.

If the cost of providing a trial version is excessive, you're likely better off negotiating a paid pilot (or paid proof of concept) of your offering (e.g., a one-year contract where they're able to cancel the contract at the end of the first month). Nothing proves a qualification than dry ink on a contract (metaphorical dry ink if you're using e-signatures). If you're unable to negotiate paid pilots for your offering, perhaps you'd better start thinking about how to lower the cost of getting a trial version out into the world.

## FREE IS GOOD WHEN IT'S NOT ME

*Practically every time a new employee in management came onboard at eSentire, the idea of a free offering was introduced by them as if we had never considered that option before. The first few times this happened I was more than somewhat irritated. However, at some point, I agreed with them, told them that it was a "capital idea," and asked if they were willing to apply that logic to their own salary. Not one person took me up on this opportunity, no matter how brilliant they had originally thought it was. Good for thee but not for me.*

Another thought: when you're pricing your offering, ensure there's a bit of wiggle room for your client to slice off (let's say 10 percent). Alternatively, you may want to include a line item that is "nice to have" but not absolutely necessary—let's consider it like an appendix as the human body can function well without one—that the potential client can turn away without pain. There are a few psychological reasons for this. First, you want to insert an additional element of control into the transaction. The client would like to maintain their upper hand in the negotiation. If and when they ask you to "sharpen your pencil," you tell them that you will take it under consideration and "I will see what I can do" to demonstrate that you want to work with them. It is not useful to take a submissive pose; you want to encourage mutual respect throughout your business dealings.

Throughout the years, I have found it counterproductive to deeply discount from your original price (assuming it is just a slightly inflated price). If you find yourself in a deeply competitive pricing environment or bid, while the temptation to discount might be great, this can ultimately lead to a "race to the bottom." Let's say that you discount your price by

50 percent. There are two negative ricochet or blowback effects. First, it signals to your potential client that you didn't put your best price forward at the outset. Second, it signals that you saw them as a sucker if they accepted. Third, it signals that you don't truly value the offering as a "premium product." Realize that your potential clients will talk—if one discovers that you offered the same product at a considerably lower price, they will quickly become angry, and you will hear about it when it comes time to renew your contract. Unless the very short-term survival of your business is at stake: Do. Not. Discount. In. A. Race. To. The. Bottom. We will return to this topic later.

Prepare for sales and pricing objections—in fact, expect them in such a manner that you role-play with someone else and have answers to the most common objections you encounter (for example, the client saying, "It's way too expensive"). You should expect to be shot down far more than welcomed with open arms (sadly, this is true for all prospects— whether customers, investors, or employees).

Afterward, let the advisor who acted as a reference know how the sales meetings went. Remember that your advisor wants to see you succeed; keep them involved in the sales process. If you do succeed in closing the sale, wow the client. Celebrate the win with your team, perform a deep dive on your sales technique and process (What worked? What didn't work?).

## FOAD PRICING

From time to time, you will come across the potential client who will require what I call the FOAD price. Just in case you weren't familiar with the acronym, FOAD stands for "fuck off and die," and FOAD pricing includes a stiff premium (e.g., 50 percent? 100 percent? Even 200 percent?) to compensate for the anticipated annoyance factor. In your lifetime, you've quite likely had to have come across truly unpleasant people, and if you're lucky, you will come to that discovery rather quickly. Undoubtedly, you will eventually be pitching your offering to one (or more) of these people. You ultimately get to decide whether you want to do business with this person and their company. If you do decide to move forward, realize that there will be unseen human costs when dealing with difficult clients which are difficult to quantify. The FOAD price is meant to alleviate some of the pain when working with what you perceive to be a particularly difficult client. Do not discount the FOAD price, but don't complain after the fact if they accept it. Rarely have I found that difficult clients at the outset are worth any premium, but you might be in survival mode where you need to bite the bullet and accept the pain. The late Anthony Bourdain felt privileged to live by what he called the "no asshole" rule—he would not work with anyone whom he deemed an asshole. You might not enjoy that particular luxury. However, sometimes the most difficult client, after significant time and positive interactions with your company, can become one of your best clients. If not, you may be lucky and discover that the client found their difficult employee whom you were dealing with to be particularly disruptive to their business and terminate their employment. In turn, you might be able to continue your business relationship afterward.

## CELEBRATE YOUR WINS

*In the early days of eSentire, when we closed a sale of any size, we would ring a cowbell and offer everyone in the office a shot of alcohol. This isn't likely sustainable in the long term. I still have the cowbell in my home office.*

In the subsequent chapters, I will elaborate on the sales process and discuss some of the metrics you should use. But first I want to dig a bit deeper into the founder-led sales psychology to get into your head and rewire your perspective.

As the founder, the onus will be on you to set direction and company tone and to explain the value of the offering (as well as the values of the company). Do not assume this will occur without considerable thought and exercise on your part. I'm going to introduce you to some of these necessary exercises and forethought.

# CHAPTER 13

# Sales Is Vulnerability

A S WE'VE SEEN, finding traction in early sales within startups is incredibly difficult. Some may say that it is the most difficult aspect of startup life throughout the first five years.

As a technical founder without sales acumen prior to my startup, I believe the following helps explain why this is so: *Sales is nothing if not vulnerability*. I would posit that we technical founders are not generally comfortable with putting ourselves in vulnerable situations, exposing ourselves, and asking for candid feedback about our creations.

But the rewards for extending yourself, for pushing through that vulnerability, are extraordinary.

First, it helps you to build empathy for those engaged in the sales process day in and day out.

The feedback that you get when you're working through the sales process includes (but is not exclusive to) building a sales funnel, tweaking the pitch message, figuring out pricing, and finessing the proper engagement of the customer. The feedback made available to you as you're working through this process is invaluable.

Second, aside from choosing the wrong cofounder, hiring the wrong salesperson is the easiest way to set back your business. Often, first-time founders have no idea what the characteristics of the right salesperson are, especially given the current place they are in their company's journey. I have seen this many times, and I have personally been guilty of it. It is my opinion that the ideal first salesperson for a startup is *not* someone with a decade or more of experience. Ideally, you want someone who is as hungry as you, with some experience selling ("dialing for dollars") as a sales development representative (SDR) but not yet burnt out. Burnout is endemic in sales, and at this early stage, you can't afford to spend the time and money on someone who's burnt out from their previous sales gig.

Ideally, their experience should be roughly analogous to your business. If they have experience selling in Big Tech (such as IBM, Google, Microsoft, or Intel), you might be tempted to bring them on board, but you should be cautious. Salespeople in Big Tech generally are given a book of business to sell offerings that are well known: they have not needed to do the "groundwork" to familiarize their target customers with their product. Find someone who has experience selling within your sphere (for example, services) in a firm that is somewhat larger than your company and entice them away. For example: if you're looking to hire your first sales development representative to lead your outbound cold-calling process, scout and hire the team lead of sales development from a company in the same or adjacent field but twice your size.

There are some people who are considered "natural sellers"; don't be taken in by their charisma. It is simply not true that "any good salesperson can sell anything."

There is also a marked difference between "inside sales" and "outside sales." "Outside sales" refers to the action of finding new customers and bringing them on board as opposed to "inside sales" to which current, existing clients are introduced to new offerings as part of an upselling process. The approaches are completely different, and most salespeople are best suited (by personality) to be in one or the other.

If you can't yet find this person, do not settle. You will need to take the reins and lead the sales process until you find the right person. You might find them in the most unlikely of places. I have often recommended scouting for the best salespeople who currently work in retail in a big-box store's tech department. You need to find someone who is coachable, who is as hungry as you are. Why are retail tech sales stores an ideal hunting ground for your first business development representative hire? They are generally young, highly motivated, and used to dealing with the public in a sales capacity. By engaging with them, you should be able to quickly get a general impression as to whether you could work with them on an ongoing basis. Keep in mind that you will be offering them a chance to take their career to the next level. I know so many people employed in successful sales management positions who started their career arc in retail tech. Remember, it is more important that you find a good fit than merely a placeholder upon whom you can shove all sales responsibility. Nobody wins when that is the case.

*The first full-time salesperson I hired came recommended by a well-respected CEO in the local software industry. The candidate had a long history of technical sales and was interested in joining us. I didn't know then what I know now. After three months onboard, he didn't seem to "click" with our current clients and hadn't brought in any sales whatsoever. He didn't help build a sales funnel, didn't have any strategy to move forward, and didn't seem to display energy or interest. He took some vacation time that he had banked, and upon his return on a Monday, I told him that I needed to see some "froth on the water." Following that little pep talk, he was a demon of activity. That week, he was making dozen' of cold calls and being exactly the salesperson we needed him to be. But early that Friday, he called in sick (an email with the phrase "sicker than my mother's old dog" if I recall correctly). Something didn't feel right—my Spidey sense was tingling. I did a little research and figured out that he was not actually sick but was, in fact, at a skiing event. I drove to the ski club only to find him—surprised—still wearing his ski gear and with ski goggles perched on the top of his head. I took his access pass from him, told him that I would meet him on Monday at 8 a.m. at a nearby coffee shop, and called the office to immediately disable all his accounts.*

*In retrospect, I see the several mistakes I made. If I had done more due diligence, I would have found that he was not historically a good salesperson—he had a history of untruths told. Further, the CEO who had referred him to us was just doing a friend a favor, and with 20/20 hindsight vision, I can intuit that he probably was just grinding out his career opportunities before retirement. This is not the kind of salesperson you need during the most critical startup stages. By the time we terminated him, we had lost months of momentum and looked more than somewhat foolish. No matter what happens, lick your wounds in private and start again. Perhaps a decade later you will be able to laugh about it.*

*What should we have done differently? We should have sampled his work product earlier (for example, from the first month). During the interview process, we should have asked him to put together what he believed an execution plan should look like from 30-, 90-, and 120-day perspectives. After he started with us, we could have been able to see how much of the sales plan had been put in place at each milestone. This emphasizes the need for regular measurement and follow-through. Then: if things weren't working out, we could pivot as appropriate, and then if it truly wasn't the right fit we could readily pull the trigger to terminate. We had abdicated the responsibility to build and adhere to an effective sales process, and we paid the painful price. We did not do that twice.*

What follows are four additional thoughts regarding sales and the growth of your sales team you should consider.

First, you need to be able to succinctly articulate your offering and its value proposition. As the founder, you need to be the *best* at doing this. If you're unable to do so, you won't be able to help instruct newly onboarded salespeople. Engage others and see what works best. Continually refine your approach. Messaging matters.

Second, especially while you are in startup mode, everyone on the team should consider themselves to be at least partially in the business of selling every single day. Note: this doesn't necessarily disappear after you graduate from startup mode and into more of a mature scale-up mode. How each employee deals with customers inexorably acts as a help or a hindrance to future sales. If you have employees working as consultants embedded into the day-to-day operations of your clients, you might find that these employees have a wide-angle view into client problems. In this way, they may be able to identify and suggest solutions that can be billed (as an upselling/internal sales effort). Given their perch, they may be in the best position to make these sales.

Third, some of the best salespeople you will find will come on recommendations made from your own happy clients. Happy clients are more likely to open their networks to you, make referrals, and act as references. Make your customers happy, and it will pay dividends for years.

Fourth (and I cannot emphasize this enough), when you hire your first salesperson, you cannot immediately abdicate your responsibility for sales. It will take time for them to understand the subtleties and intricacies of your product or offering. You may need to make many "four-legged sales calls" where you accompany them on their first meetings or while working the booth at conferences. If, as a technical founder (and especially as a developer), you are familiar with the concept of "pair programming," then you will immediately understand this in a sales context. At some point, your new hire will be able to ride without training wheels but don't expect it to happen quickly.

*I was working with a first-time cofounder who was struggling with closing sales for their cybersecurity services offering. None of this is uncommon, so I asked about their current sales process. Several months ago, they had found a salesperson who had significant experience as an account executive at a large, publicly traded cybersecurity product company but had been recently terminated. They came on board to lead the sales efforts for this startup. The individual's personal compensation was more than what the two cofounders were paying themselves, plus the person had demanded access to a full enterprise client database account to help with sales prospecting (at a retail cost of $50,000 per year), had not yet made a single sale, and was, remarkably, starting to ask about bonuses.*

*There were several causes for concern here.*

*To be sure, cybersecurity sales can be a tough endeavor, since, in the end, you're selling <u>trust</u>. However, it was my belief that there were several mismatches in this hire.*

*First, the new account executive wasn't necessarily set up to fail, they were definitely not set up to succeed. To start, they probably weren't the "best fit" match for each other. It is a difficult transition from a well-funded, publicly traded company to a lean (some may say starving) startup with negligible marketing support.*

*Second, the cofounders admitted that they were relieved to relinquish the sales efforts to someone else. They abdicated all sales efforts (for better or for worse) to the new employee. There was little in the way of assistance including understanding their market, their approach, or possible verticals to investigate. It was truly a sink-or-swim method of sales. If you've never had to "start from zero" as a salesperson without supporting marketing collateral, a starting sales pitch, marketing qualified leads or sales qualified leads (MQLs or SQLs) sales can be an incredibly intimidating task.*

*Third, there was no sales plan in place regarding lead generation, sales funnel, or sales engineering efforts. As there was no plan, there was no way to measure success other than asking, "Did you sell anything?" as there were no performance indicators, there was no way to set specific goals (including a formal sales funnel), and nobody asked for regular updates.*

*Fourth, the purchase of the expensive corporate client database subscription at full retail price underlined the fact that this poor account executive didn't know exactly how to move forward. They might have had access to this database at their previous job and thought that perhaps this could show initiative and shine a beacon on how to secure sales. As a startup, if you haven't figured out who your ideal client is yet, using a broad shotgun tool like an enterprise client database probably isn't going to help you.*

*Fifth, many months went by without this sales executive making a single sale. Without assuming malice on the part of the salesperson, this must have been excruciating for him. In the meantime, the two cofounders quietly burned inside: "Why isn't this guy bringing in the sales?" At some point, the salesperson likely thought they'd "double down," go for broke, and ask for compensation sweeteners to go along with any sale.*

*So, best to address the core issues. Accept the fact that the founders need to take a significant part of the blame: they wholly abdicated the responsibility for sales to someone ill-suited to take charge of that task. I suggested that instead of mining the enterprise database, they work their personal connections (for example, by leveraging LinkedIn) and start looking for people they'd worked with previously to start making referrals. I suggested that, instead of relying on a seasoned (perhaps over-seasoned) sales professional from a large product company, take a different tactic. As stated earlier, find a few companies in a similar field that are a bit larger than you are (say twenty-five employees to your ten) and find the SDR who's been there for a couple of years—perhaps the person was promoted to become the SDR team lead. Reach out to them and see if they'd be interested in joining your startup. Obviously, you'll need to figure out what would incentivize them to leave their current position.*

*Alternatively, I suggested that they make a few trips to a specific tech retail store and talk to a few of the sales representatives on the floor. Get their email contacts, have a breakfast or coffee meeting with them, and see if they'd be interested.*

*I warned them that in either case, if they found a suitable candidate, they still would not be able to wholly abdicate the role of client education and sales. It would still be of incredibly high importance for them to have visibility into the sales funnel—even more so now after they had spent several months learning a valuable lesson.*

*In a subsequent meeting, I discovered that they had released the "seasoned" sales executive from that specific duty and had taken my advice and thereafter hired an energetic former retail tech salesperson who was (in their words) "killing it." This was a better fit, and they emerged as wiser cofounders in support of their new employee.*

There are many outsourcing companies that will perform your "dialing for dollars" early sales outreach efforts. Should you enlist the services of outsourced early business development representatives, you would purchase customer lists (culled from conference attendance and credential opt-in data), create a sales script, and let them begin the process. But I do not recommend this—for several reasons.

First, the odds of success are terribly slim. Unsolicited inbound sales queries (whether by email, phone call, or LinkedIn) are a series of daily tsunamis to everyone—and generally regarded by sales prospects as only slightly better than call center employees selling duct-cleaning services. The sales results are demoralizing.

Second, the employees of the outsourcing company are not generally well seasoned. Any competent outsourced SDR will quickly be able to find a more stable and long-term sales position somewhere else.

Third, if, by chance, a party is interested in further details immediately (also known as a "hot lead'), the outsourced employee is unable to engage deeper. They then must let them off the hook and arrange for a deeper conversation with a more senior salesperson later. And yet, with this kind of process in place, you lose the momentum of a sale.

For raw early business development outreach, if you're not going to do it yourself, you're better off finding your own junior employee and spend the time training them to get them up to speed.

There are many other subtle intricacies of the sales process. You will find, as you expand, that facets of sales including geography, cultural differences, and implicit cultural bias will loom large in sales prospecting and sales activities. Don't expect one salesperson to be a chameleon able to morph into a sales superhero in each situation.

How should you compensate your salespeople? With tongue firmly half-planted in cheek, I often say that salespeople are "coin-operated": they are primarily incentivized by money. There isn't anything wrong with that. Recall that nobody is going to love "your baby" as much as you do, and you must realize that although you might have entirely altruistic intentions, not everyone else will be similarly positioned.

Sales compensation generally consists of a base salary, expenses, and commission. I have never seen a successful salesperson work on commission only. I would be highly skeptical of anyone who was happy to get a job wholly dependent on commission; that person is most likely to leave at the first chance they receive a different job offer.

Sales are heart-wrenchingly difficult, and the challenge is accentuated by the fact that success and failure are easily calculable: "How much did you close this quarter?" "Did you reach your target?" At the end of the quarter, the odometer is reset back to zero.

Not every company's sales environment is like that portrayed in the David Mamet play, *Glengarry Glen Ross*, but there are definite pressures that all salespeople feel. As a result, after years in the salt mines, sales professionals are excellent candidates for burnout. The stress from "not making your numbers" can lead to alcoholism, drug abuse, gambling, and other addictions.

Keep in mind that your startup will simply not survive without sales. As a founder (particularly if your personality tends toward that of introversion), you might find sales distasteful at the outset, but you will need to become comfortable with playing a significant role in sales engineering, messaging, and execution. Adhering to a founder-led sales process is necessary, or you will flounder until your startup dies.

# CHAPTER 14

# Demand Generation— Filling the Sales Funnel

T HIS IS A GOOD time to describe the "sales funnel." The stages of the sales funnel are as follows:

1. Awareness
2. Interest
3. Consideration
4. Decision
5. Purchase

Ideally, unqualified prospects enter the top of the funnel, follow a qualifying process (they are marketing qualified or sales qualified), are persuaded to commit, and finally sign a contract and purchase. But how do you find prospects who might be interested in what you offer? These prospects populate what is referred to as the "top of the funnel."

There are several ways to generate leads for the top of the funnel.

First, seek out qualified leads through your network of advisors or trusted partners. As an early-stage company, the most effective leads you will find are those made through this critical core in your network. A personal introduction carries significant weight and can help bypass an overzealous gatekeeper. When advisors offer an introduction, realize that they are staking their reputations on your behalf. Be especially mindful of this trust that has been extended to you. I will discuss formal partnership arrangements later.

How can you best harness the social capital gained through advisors or trusted partners? LinkedIn provides some tooling to help mine your network to calculate social proximity. Let's first define what LinkedIn means by social proximity: in short—what is the distance between you and your ideal client, target buyer, or ultimate decision maker? For the sake of brevity, I will just define close social proximity as land from which you can farm for your ideal client.

Best case: You are directly connected (first-degree connection) to your ideal client. This person already has accepted a connection with you, so the first and most difficult step has been achieved. It is important that once you've made this connection, you do not immediately jump into a heavy-handed sales pitch. Depending on the person, you may find yourself immediately sidelined from the LinkedIn conversation, your target seemingly disappearing into thin air as they have blocked you.

Next best case: You are directly connected (first-degree connection) to an advisor or trusted partner who is directly connected to your ideal client, also known as a second-degree connection.

Next best case: You have a second-degree connection to your ideal client through a LinkedIn connection who isn't an advisor or trusted partner.

Next best case: You are separated by three or more degrees from your ideal client. This is by far the least valuable category and will require significant effort on your part.

LinkedIn provides excellent tooling to search for people using filters for varying criteria. Starting with "Companies" and "People," you can then filter for first- and second-degree connections and filter further through "Location" and "Title" as appropriate. Through this query-filtering system, you may be able to start building out your ideal client list as you identify people's names, companies, titles, and connection proximity.

Remember, in the search for your ideal client, do not burn the social capital of your advisors and trusted partners. I have had people I have never actually met in real life (or online) send me LinkedIn introductions and, upon accepting them, have asked if I would be a reference for them to one of my connections. That is not ideal.

Second, conduct outbound electronic queries and calling campaigns, including but not necessarily exclusive to email, cold-calling, and using LinkedIn. Though you can research and assemble your own list of possible customers, dozens of companies sell contact lists culled from previous conference events. Typically, junior sales staff (SDRs) will be given a subset of the large list and, ideally, qualify the list with a bit of research and then send the prospects a targeted message with the intent to pique their interest. As much as unsolicited spam email is annoying, it remains one of the most effective marketing tools; be careful not to contravene domicile-specific anti-SPAM laws that may carry punitive fines.

Phone calls (aka "dialing for dollars") follow a similar guidebook. However, keep in mind that your targeted recipients are well guarded against inbound sales calls by caller ID and protective executive assistants as it is not unusual for them to receive at least a dozen unsolicited calls daily. I highly recommend that you avoid calling people on their personal cell phone as little else raises the same amount of ire from sales prospects.

Third, the use of free trials can present an excellent inbound stream of opportunity for the top of the sales funnel. As I've explicitly stated earlier in this book, I'm not a fan of leaving money on the table, so the most important factors in the use of a free trial period are three-fold. First, ensure that there is sufficient functionality enabled for the interested party to fully exercise and fall in love with your offering. Second, ensure that it is time-limited so that its use isn't forever; depending on the sophistication of the product offering you may need to go beyond the typical two- to four-week trial period. Third, ensure that the client feedback data that your team gathers from the trials is put to good use. You will need to follow up throughout (and especially at the end of) the trial period to gather usage data, determine if the client sufficiently found value and why and what features they found most valuable, and prepare for roadblocks to a paid engagement. Often these early demo users are reluctant to escape from the shadows of internet semi-anonymity, but you will need to encourage them to share their thoughts. The data you gather from actual usage by prospects can be invaluable in your marketing endeavors and future pipeline. When discussing these products with prospects, feel free to ask the user if there's someone else they know within their network who could find this interesting or useful. As a subtle form of implied reciprocity, they should give you their impressions, feedback, and advice in return for using your offering.

Fourth, trade shows (onsite or virtual) and seminars can be excellent methods for customer outreach. There's little value in merely putting up a booth, printing marketing collateral, cobbling together some branded swag, and then waiting for the chance for customers to come visit you. Ideally, you will need to do significant research beforehand to identify potential customers and partners. Your outbound research can be used to see if your target customers will be in attendance. And try to set up meetings in advance. Seminars you may wish to set up adjacent to large trade shows can help elicit warm sales opportunities once attendees have been qualified.

Trade shows can be very expensive, and the ROI hurdle can be significant, so choose your trade shows carefully. Often at large trade shows, there are deals that are available for startups: smaller booths, in a specific area often called something like "startup alley" with a smaller price tag. Some of the most innovative offerings come from companies in that category. Keep track of these leads; they will need to be qualified and added to the sales funnel as appropriate. At the same time, beware of "tradeshow fever," where everyone seems extremely friendly and eminently qualified to purchase while on the tradeshow floor. That exuberance is often fleeting, so don't be disappointed that there is a significant drop-off in interest once the conference closes. It is critical that you engage these contacts that you've gathered: they were very expensive to obtain.

Recognize that not all meetups, conferences, and trade shows will provide the same level of value. Ideally, you want to go where the best quality of potential ideal clients will be. I have found from decades of experience that it is unlikely that your local Chamber of Commerce monthly small business meetups can assemble those ideal clients. These meetups can be fun from a social perspective, especially if you're looking to meet others in the community. However, I have found that so many of these events have the same attendees repeatedly. I have referred to these attendees who don't seem to be making any significant movement forward as "cheese eaters" because it appears that these free outreach events form the entirety of their social calendar! They put on a collared shirt, munch on some stale crackers, and cheese that's drying up; drink a couple of plastic wine glasses of flat wine; maybe schmooze a little bit before the main event speaker presents; and then dart home. If this is what you like, enjoy it purely as a social endeavor, but don't fool yourself into thinking this is a serious sales activity.

Similarly, if you only go to meetups or conferences that are of interest to you (and not where your ideal clients gather), this can be detrimental to your direct sales success. It may be immensely valuable for you to present there to help establish yourself as a subject matter expert (which can help you as you move forward), but unless you sit squarely in your own target market, this is not where your ideal clients are. Get out of your bubble, go to where they are—you will need to do some more research to find out where they prefer to go to find new ideas or solutions.

Fifth, requests for proposals (RFPs) are inbound requests to reply to the specific needs of a company or government or NGO client. Generally, the clients have assembled this document of solution-set needs to be sent out broadly to elicit responses. There is no guarantee that you will pass the first hurdle or even that the project itself will be undertaken. From a startup perspective, the pursuit of RFPs can be extremely time-consuming and expensive. Often the most important parameter is price, and you don't want to be caught in a "race to the bottom." As such, unless you have played a part in writing or providing input into the RFP, then you probably shouldn't expect to win it.

There are also well-established old-school (we might call them "analog") and somewhat more conventional and passive methods to fill your sales funnel. As the market continues to evolve, especially in the post-COVID-19 lockdown world, there is a benefit in taking advantage of technology and finding ways to broaden your reach to win customers. These newer methodologies (let's call them "leveraged digital") demand that you establish yourself as a thought leader and expand your reach through those vectors. What follows are some examples of leveraged digital initiatives.

One example is to regularly write a long-form blog post that educates the target market on some problem that your solution solves. Offer tangible benefits (i.e., takeaways) best targeted to your ideal buyer. Do not insult your readership (with buzzword bingo), and most importantly, do not hard-sell your solution within these blog posts. Thought leadership pieces that I have personally written include the following:

1. How to prepare your firm to answer the Securities and Exchange Commission's (SEC) cybersecurity questions.
2. A complete information security policy "starter bundle" framework upon which companies could build their own procedure manual.
3. A complete incident-response playbook framework detailing terminology, responsibilities, and specific actions to take depending on the attack vector(s).

Ensure that there is value given freely.

Another approach is to offer a series of interviews (for example, in webinar format) with certain of your clients to succinctly describe how you solved their problem, how easy it is to work with you, and how much time they saved by using your solution. Use all appropriate social media platforms to publicize these interviews.

When you find specific content that seems to have traction, only *then* spend ad money to amplify its reach and impact online.

What all these observations have taught me is that the sales process requires fealty to a scientific methodology. Without rigor, it will flounder or fail outright. Spend time and energy on those approaches that have demonstrated some success, as I've detailed in this chapter, and then use time and tenacity to amplify your reach.

# CHAPTER 15

# Sales Metrics

N O MATTER WHAT CHANNEL you ultimately use when bringing on your first full-time salesperson, you need to set targets and track metrics. "What gets measured gets managed" is a fragment of the phrase attributed to management guru Peter Drucker. The full phrase is "What gets measured gets managed even when it is pointless to measure and manage it, and even if it harms the purpose of the organization to do so." So, when you're tracking your sales metrics and setting targets, be mindful that the intent isn't merely to "make the metrics look good." Sales outcomes are the most important data to track, and the intent behind gathering and managing sales metrics is to identify trends and show progress against targets.

As a broad guide, HubSpot, the very popular customer relationship management (CRM) software, defines the sales stages as follows:

- Lead
- Qualified
- Proof of value planned
- Proof of value

- Negotiation
- Closed won/lost

What sales metrics are the most important? Which sales metrics are necessary?

You may want to choose a combination of metrics through three different broad categories: sales activity metrics (leading indicators to qualify leads into the funnel), sales performance metrics (indicators of qualified leads within the funnel), and customer satisfaction metrics (trailing indicators to show customer health).

Sales activity metrics may include the following (I suggest these be tracked, reviewed, and updated on a weekly basis):

- Outbound phone calls made
- Emails sent
- LinkedIn network invitations sent
- LinkedIn InMail messages sent

Sales performance metrics may include the following (I suggest that these also be tracked, reviewed, and updated on a weekly basis):

- Percentage of phone calls accepted and resulting in a follow-up meeting
- Email click-through rate (CTR)
- Email response (positive)
- Percentage of LinkedIn connections accepted
- LinkedIn InMail reply rate

Derived from these previous metrics, the following metrics will help you identify the quality of leads in your sales funnel and, accordingly, can impact your revenue. (I suggest that these results be collated and reviewed on a monthly basis—and that they be folded up into a final number at the end of each quarter):

- Number of deals in sales funnel
- Percentage of sales qualified leads
- Total number of opportunities
- Percentage of quota attainment
- Number of closed deals
- Conversion rate
- Win rate
- Average sales cycle length
- Average deal size
- Number of upsells
- Customer lifetime value (CLV)
- Monthly recurring revenue (MRR)
- Annual recurring revenue (ARR)
- Average revenue per customer
- Total revenue

These metrics will serve multiple strategic benefits. Perhaps unsurprisingly, you will find that many of these metrics are of interest to potential investors. We will expand on these (and more) in that chapter as appropriate.

Avoid trumpeting or chasing metrics that don't matter, including vanity metrics. Vanity metrics may include figures that are deceiving or not fundamentally important to your success. A few suggestions might include cumulative sales, website clicks, and the number of company LinkedIn followers. Find what "golden metrics" exist as appropriate to your vertical and tweak as appropriate.

What I hope I've shown in this chapter is that sales is a numbers game and it requires consistent measurement, or else you will not understand what efforts are successful or falling short. Metrics might not tell the entire story, but they can help measure and gauge progress. Keep track.

# CHAPTER 16

# Sales Discovery and Development

THE EARLY SALES DISCOVERY calls are the most difficult. One question that frequently arises after some small improvements in the sales engagement process is "How can I determine that my contact is the decision maker?" It is a tricky situation. Ideally, you'll want to engage with your prospect, but there are times that they don't have the political (or financial) capital to sign the deal. They often are reticent to reveal this, too.

Do you find that there are questions you pose that they can't answer? If you ask them, "Who in your company is directly affected by this problem (that you solve)?" Is it them? If it is someone else, you should suggest that perhaps they be included in the next call (i.e., a demo). This can be a delicate dance because you don't want to undermine the goodwill you have built with this initial person.

If you find that they demur, it may be because they don't yet want to introduce you to the ultimate decision-maker for a few reasons. First, you may not have yet demonstrated that you are sufficiently trustworthy or have enough credibility. Second, they may not believe that a more powerful decision-maker needs to be involved at this point. Third, they may know that the decision-maker explicitly does not want to be involved.

At this point, it may be best to exercise radical candor and explicitly refer to this unresolved situation. After "dancing" around this topic for some time, you can tactfully state the obvious and call out their unwillingness to close the deal:

> We've spent several weeks working on this project and ultimately, I need to see if the timing is right for us to work together. At this point, I haven't yet been introduced to your CTO and I'm not sure why—but I can guess. Either I haven't earned the credibility you need to be comfortable with such an introduction, you don't believe that your CTO needs to be involved in this decision, or they simply don't want to be involved. Can you tell me which it is?

If you're able to remain empathetic and tactful, they should appreciate your candor. You can't keep sales leads open forever. If they can't help to connect you with the ultimate party with signoff authority, it may be for the best to put this specific lead on the back burner and move on to other appealing opportunities.

At times their intentions are not benign: some people just want to waste your time or use you to make them feel more important.

After a successful client acquisition process, customer satisfaction metrics should be gathered and gauged through customer surveys to obtain a customer satisfaction score (CSAT) and net promoter score (NPS). Ideally, you want to regularly schedule these surveys to identify possible problems and, ultimately, help increase the stickiness of your offering among your client base. Ideally, these scores (if positive) can be used within your marketing collateral to demonstrate your clout and credibility in the market.

The top of your sales funnel needs to be many times larger than the workload you can support; generally, it needs to be at least five times bigger and often more (depending on the length of time it takes for an interested potential client to execute a contract).

How can you help speed up that process to a contractual sale? Again, you need to put yourself in your client's shoes—with their perspective, make the sales process as frictionless as possible to gain interest and engage with you.

One further thing to note that may be obvious in retrospect: time kills all deals. If you're a technical founder who's been more comfortable in resolving bugs in code bases or developing new functionality, you might not recognize this. Sales leads, like fruit on the vine, can rot. The Jira ticket upon which you need to react—I'm referring here to the project management software tool—might still be there in a week. Meanwhile, a client waiting for a contract (from your nonexistent sales administrator) may consider waiting for your response a fruitless endeavor and move on, possibly to a competitor. You may never get the opportunity to make up for this lost ground. Even if you have a hot qualified lead with an internal champion on your side, there are ample opportunities for things to go awry. Your champion may get demoted or fired or even leave the company and then you may be back to the earliest stages.

## SALES ENGINEERING BUILDING BLOCKS: REVENUE, EXPANSION/ UPSELL, MARGIN, CHURN

Can you succinctly describe your offering? Do you understand the benefits that your offering can bring to your potential client? Can you quantify the direct value?

The primary benefits typically associated with any offering are the ability to save the client money (cost-effectiveness), provide an improved outcome, or deliver results more quickly. This is an adjacent idea to the "Iron Triangle" concept: "You can have it fast, you can have it cheap, or you can have it good: pick two." Within which of these categories does your offering reside?

In general, much of technical sales engineering (especially when describing cybersecurity products) is more difficult than that of a material product. What are some of the reasons it is so difficult?

First, the offering will undoubtedly be unable to address all conceivable concerns. While human needs are finite and can be clearly defined, human wants are limitless and insatiable. There will always be client itches that cannot be scratched, let alone soothed. Once problems are solved (or at least remedied), new ones will crop up that cannot be solved (either partially or wholly) by the same original solution.

Second, the offering might be ephemeral. For example, what is "security?" I'm not asking this from a purely philosophical perspective, but rather from one rooted in *terra firma*. When pitching an offering, you'll need to draw analogies for the customer to grasp. The more concrete the analogy, the easier it will be for your potential customer to understand. However, analogies are slippery by their very definition, and when you're describing an ephemeral state or item in concrete terms, you'll never find an exact match that resonates readily. In a similar vein, you may find that both the marketing and sales departments (both your own and your competition's) may not present the facts in an entirely truthful or accurate manner. Engineers may cringe or shudder at this. There are empirical methods used to measure and gauge ephemeral phenomena (including cybersecurity exposure and risk, actuarial tables, and credit scores). But historically, the use of analogies wins over pure numbers in business.

A recent example of this may be found in the competition between the firewall manufacturers Fortinet and Palo Alto Networks. They both created an appliance that handles network traffic to segregate the "dangerous side" (the internet) from the "safe side" (the internal network). Fortinet had an early head-start with its hardware, using application-specific integrated circuit (ASIC) technology to interpret and categorize threats faster than if it were done using software alone. Fortinet used the term "unified threat management" to distinguish its product line with exacting precision. Let's call this marketing approach "speeds and feeds": Fortinet would have a clean table describing the product model, what network speeds it was appropriate to handle, how many interfaces were available, and if the model was best suited for home, small office, mid-sized business, enterprise, or utility networks. However, Palo Alto Networks burst onto the scene with a similar hardware proposition, but instead of focusing on the empirical data, it revealed its value proposition as an "outcome-driven warm story" to describe how the end user would be better protected. Palo Alto Networks also defined itself as a "Next-Generation Firewall" (NGFW) to further distinguish itself from the last generation. Palo Alto Networks exploded with success. Fortinet continues to compete with Palo Alto Networks, but Fortinet has not been able to regain the ground it lost.

Third, in that same vein, clients within any market may get obsessed with what is known as "shiny object syndrome." Any new entrant to the market with a flashy new perspective can attract attention momentarily whether the offering accomplishes what it purports to do or not. The reframing of "what a firewall does" as described in the previous paragraph demonstrated exactly that.

Fourth, the nature of competition will eventually act in the manner of a school of fish. Competitors carefully watch each other, and if something new seems to work, they shamelessly copy competitors' verbiage, phrasing, acronyms, tone, and even color palettes from each other's websites. Eventually, competitors begin to congregate and move in a seemingly similar direction en masse.

## THE BIRTH OF THE MANAGED DETECTION AND RESPONSE CATEGORY

*My own personal example of market messaging involves the transition from "managed security services provider" (MSSP) to "managed detection and response" (MDR). Many years ago, an analyst from a very well-known technology advisory firm whose name starts with the letter "G" visited eSentire and spent an afternoon with us. An analyst report from this G-named company that goes public to clients can catapult a startup's visibility to the broader customer marketplace. Over the course of that afternoon, the analyst heard what we were doing and then tried to persuade us that we should be part of its MSSP category chart. I demurred, saying, "I know what variables are used to determine whether a company should be included in the MSSP category. That includes how many firewalls we manage and how many VPN concentrators we manage. We don't do any of that, and we might never do that." The analyst was surprised and asked for clarification. I said,*

*We are looking for the attacks that made their way through all the infosec infrastructure—whether it is firewalls, antivirus, antispam, VPN connectivity—whatever the client uses. We seek to detect those unwanted inbound attacks and kick them out—proactively if possible. We want to have as much valuable data available at our fingertips to investigate an attack while it is happening, and then respond to evict the undesirable entity.*

*We were calling it "collabritive threat management" or "micro-incident resposnse handling," but a few months later, the definition of MDR was listed with a half-dozen similar companies (eSentire was prominently featured in the new report by the analyst at G). A year later, there were dozens of MDR companies listed in the updated report. They were mostly MSSPs that had rebranded themselves with the new moniker while nothing else within their service offering had changed.*

Ultimately, the broader market, once aligned to some semblance of a base offering or description, will engage in a pricing model that I will refer to again as a "race to the bottom." What was originally a premium offering is standardized and/or diluted to emerge as the cheapest offering to squeeze the last few dollars out of the market by any means necessary. Often this appeals to the least-educated consumer who does not have sufficient expertise to tell the difference among competitors. By way of analogy, if your potential customer doesn't know the difference between a cheap off-the-rack suit and bespoke tailoring, it may be an uphill battle to demonstrate the distinctions between the two suits. It may be that the customer prefers a cheap suit to no suit at all.

So, given these distractions, how do you stand out (and ahead of your competition)? How can you frame your offering (from a marketing perspective) to differentiate yourself?

So much of the information security sales process revolves around creating FUD: "fear, uncertainty, and doubt." Historically, it has been as effective in selling cybersecurity in the same manner that overt sexuality has helped in selling alcohol and perfume.

However, I find that these days clients are exhausted by the traditional go-to of using FUD to sell cybersecurity offerings. My preference is to focus on the positive benefits of our offerings to accelerate a customer's business goals—and customers tell me this is a refreshing change from the doom and gloom perspectives used by competitors.

What are some positive aspects you should employ when selling cybersecurity services and/or products? These aspects may, I feel, resonate with any technical offering for any tech startup. The four positive aspects upon which I would like to primarily focus to demonstrate value to a potential customer are visibility, insight, control, and outcome (VICO, for short).

First, visibility. When dealing with the properties of ephemeral goods, providing visibility into processes or behaviors that previously were unavailable or outright invisible is an attractive and positive way to describe value.

Second, insight. Where visibility can provide access to raw data, insight can help provide context into that raw data to glean valuable information from which to enable the business to make better decisions.

Third, control. When a risk is ephemeral in nature, anything that can help improve the business' control over its real effects is both positive and valuable.

Fourth, outcome. When you combine the three previous aspects you can start to create a better description of what a final positive outcome is for the potential customer.

Again, resist the urge to focus on the "fear, uncertainty, and doubt" mode of evangelizing your offering. The last thing you want to do is come across as if you're selling "asshole insurance," since your customers will recoil at any such insinuation.

In summary, fill your sales funnel by identifying your ideal client, really listening and hearing their needs, and focusing on delivering a solution using positive messaging.

## KEEP IN MIND: YOU'RE PLANNING AN END GAME

All this while, you have steeled yourself to the realities of startup life, and with clear eyes, you've dedicated yourself to survive those most difficult initial years. Along with the business steps needed to grow your firm, you're planning out your survival tactics, and you now have a better (though perhaps still quite rough) idea of how much time you want to commit to your new company and define what would be an "ideal" exit.

The endgame strategies you deploy will differ significantly under the following different commercial mega-success scenarios you might envision:

1. Sell your company at a $50 million USD valuation in two years.
2. Stay private but achieve a billion-dollar valuation in five years.
3. Go public at a multibillion-dollar valuation in ten years.
4. Sell your company when you're ready to retire in twenty years.

Any of these outcomes or exit strategies are amazing, and which one is best depends on you and your wishes. You can change exit strategies midstream, but you'll probably have a more satisfying outcome if you can at least paint the broad strokes in advance. In the words of the Cheshire cat, if you don't know where you're going, any road will get you there. That is likely a suboptimal way of planning for success, however. And it may be premature and grandiose to think that you could secure a fraction of the success envisioned in any one of these four imagined success scenarios. You need to keep level-headed and focused on the prize. So, to help you think rationally about your future, let's start looking, in the next chapter, into the coalface of the biggest stumbling blocks to your growth as you transition from startup to scale-up modes.

# CHAPTER 17

# How to Compete against Larger Competitors

---

*When starting eSentire in 2001, there weren't a lot of managed information security service companies in business. Three that spring to mind were LURHQ, Counterpane, and Secureworks. LURHQ was founded in 1996 while Counterpane and Secureworks were both founded in 1999. Each of these companies was very well respected. They were founded and supported by information-security luminaries. As one example, Counterpane was cofounded by Bruce Schneier, a well-published cryptography expert, once described as a "security guru" by* the Economist. *In 2006, Counterpane was acquired by BT Group (aka British Telecom).*

*In 2006, LURHQ was subsumed under merger into Secureworks to create a powerhouse-managed security information and security services entity. In 2011, Dell announced that it would acquire Secureworks to become a part of Dell Services. It became a publicly traded company in 2016 although it is still majority-owned by Dell.*

*Imagine competing against Michael Dell. Multibillionaire Michael Dell. Twenty-fourth richest man in the world Michael Dell.*

*I am living proof that it is possible to compete against much larger companies with much deeper, unfathomably large pockets. Much larger companies must deal with problems that you don't have—yet. Public companies have a spotlight put on them like you wouldn't believe. Short sellers watch like hungry hawks for signs of weakness. They need to deal with a demanding client base, significant technical debt, employees that might not have the same "hunger" you do, power struggles, compliance costs, public relations risks if an executive trips up in a public meeting, and the acute, almost paranoid understanding that past success does not guarantee a bright future.*

ERE'S HOW YOU CAN beat them.

First, silently give gratitude to larger competitors that have paved the way before you. They've been able to educate the market for the need for the specific offering. It is now up to you to detail the differences between your offerings and to identify your strengths.

Second, *never* denigrate your competitors outright, especially if the potential customer doesn't know about them. Give no energy to them; your sales and positioning are simply about your team and your offering, not theirs.

Third, focus on the advantages that you have versus the more entrenched competition. For example, you are agile. You can make decisions faster. You can give your clients direct access to make suggestions to improve and adjust your product pipeline.

Fourth, never project neediness. Even if you desperately need the business, never explicitly state this. Remember that the person to whom you're pitching your offering wants to feel secure in their choice—it must not reflect poorly on them and their career arc if they say "yes" to you. If they sense that you're on the edge of corporate collapse, it will not endear them to you.

You don't have to gain much of the big players' market share—you only need to peel off a small percentage from them to be successful. What might seem like a rounding error to their bottom line can significantly change yours.

After a certain point, if you can successfully chip away at their client base, you will find yourself on their radar. This isn't absolutely a bad thing. You should expect that they may start to make erratic moves in response. If they're not able to successfully respond to your agility in filling their product gaps, they will undoubtedly move to the easy button of "race to the bottom" by reducing their price, often drastically. As I've stated several times, this is not a race you want to find yourself in. If you position yourself as a premium product or offering, you'll need to stay firm and persevere.

*There was one potential client engagement where we were competing against a considerably larger competitor; we had successfully completed a head-to-head proof of concept (PoC), had met the success criteria the client had defined, and were confident with our results and the superiority of our offering. We found out that our original pricing was roughly the same but that our competitor had dropped its price 50 percent from the original price and the client was asking if we were willing to sharpen our pencils to match it. I suggested to our team that we drop our price by 5 percent.*

*We won the deal.*

*I had surmised that the client, when seeing that the company was willing to cut its price in half, would have put in their mind that our so-called competitor was taking them to be "suckers" if they'd have agreed with their original pricing. I was correct. Stick to your guns as the premium offering and don't be condescending to your client base.*

*As a final addendum, in 2017, that same competitor made an offer to purchase eSentire for nine digits of USD. We turned it down to accept another bid.*

By positioning yourself as that premium offering, you may find that you will become a particularly attractive employer, and former employees from your behemoth competitors will be interested in your solution. This provides you an excellent opportunity to improve the bench strength of your team. Avail yourself of the knowledge that these people bring to you regarding your competition's strategies and approaches (while always keeping mindful of any nondisclosure agreements that may be in force).

There is a book called *Rogue Waves: Future-Proof Your Business to Survive and Profit from Radical Change* written by futurist Jonathan Brill. He posits that "rogue waves" are a natural extension of Harvard economist Michael E. Porter's "market forces" and of the "blue vs. red ocean" theories I've noted earlier, since these waves typically consist of an aggregation of small forces that suddenly overwhelm their targets. Brill's book is akin to an instruction manual for how existing companies can defend themselves against these rogue waves. I personally believe that startups should position themselves as the rogue waves themselves, preparing to do battle against much larger competitors.

If you are successful in clawing away employees, customers, and market share from your competitors, you may discover that the rogues begin to investigate your company as an acquisition target. Approach these inbound queries with caution—what might look like due diligence sessions with the intent to acquire you may only be a fact-finding mission where your competition now has access to your "special sauce," underlying business processes, product pipeline, and customer list. It is rational to be paranoid in the world of tech startups, and irrational not to be, especially when you're gaining traction.

## DAVID VERSUS SLIGHTLY LARGER DAVID (UNFUNDED STARTUP VERSUS FUNDED STARTUP) DURING THE 2023 GLOBAL MACRO INSANITY

*The challenge of startup survival in 2023 was nothing like I had seen in my three-decade-plus working career. The valuations of public technology companies significantly dropped; companies that went public through the days of SPAC frenzy found their valuations practically bottom out. In the private market, companies that were able to raise early rounds with comparative ease were finding themselves in treacherous waters as they pivoted from a "grow-at-all-costs" strategy to a "get-to EBITDA-positive" mode.*

*One founder, at an info-security startup in the early stages of raising a priced equity round, lamented the fact that its closest competition had raised $10 million USD in 2021 with an inferior product but that the due diligence his startup was currently involved in was unfair by comparison. Just as the public capital markets in 2023 were in a funk, this was also the case in the private startup market. Fewer investors, despite having "dry powder" cash, were in any rush to invest during this macroeconomic malaise.*

*One specific point of solace I noted to him: the competition might have raised a healthy amount of capital, but it had some serious problems as a result. First, just because you're well funded, it doesn't mean that sales will follow. Everyone is fighting the same global macroeconomic madness. If the offering doesn't meet anyone's needs, it will be difficult to sell. Second, the clock is ticking on that investment. The investors did not simply donate money to the company—they wanted to see a return, and the sooner the better. Finally, every three months, the board of directors formally meets, and believe me: they carefully examine the sales numbers and compare them to the projections made at the beginning of the quarter. If the sales figures presented are well above quota, you can bet that the next quarter's quotas will be adjusted up significantly. However, if sales quotas aren't being met, there are difficult and uncomfortable questions being asked regarding product-market fit and personnel competency. During difficult economic conditions, it is difficult to make a persuasive case for retaining sales personnel who are not performing to plan.*

*Do not assume that funding solves all issues. Keep to your own knitting, "embrace the suck," and get out of there and grow your business.*

Always remember that larger, deeper-pocketed competitors have paved the way for your success. Respect that. You can compete by addressing their faults but do not underestimate them. Deeply investigate your larger competition and turn your weaknesses into strengths. Agility beats inertia. Bespoke offerings can outperform mass-produced products. Be focused, not generalized. You have a new product versus their technical debt. Be David versus Goliath. Be absolutely ruthless when dealing with your competition, give them no ground, and grant them no assistance whatsoever. Be the persistent mosquito that will not give up until you're swatted into mush. Be the small bird of promise that chases and attacks the much larger hawk who lives in fear.

# CHAPTER 18

# Modes to Grow
# Your Business

F ROM WHAT I CAN see, there are four general routes to growing
your business.

## ORGANIC GROWTH

If you're reading this book, it's likely that you're in serious startup mode
and you've not yet raised a Series A funding round. You might even
be in a situation where you've not yet made any revenue (i.e., you are
"pre-rev"). Some startups have been able to raise a surprising amount
of money pre-revenue based on the strength of the team and/or the
offering (and were able to benefit from favorable global macroeconomic
conditions for lenders and investors, notably, very low interest rates).
These startups usually receive an inordinate amount of media coverage
and, consequently, more mindshare in the startup community. They are
the broad exception, and those sources of funding often dry up when
economic conditions degrade, as we witnessed in 2023.

Organic growth refers to your ability to work your network to make sales, find true believers, and capitalize on the information obtained during this process. Statistically, this is the most likely way that you will be able to grow your startup.

The very best way to grow revenue is by establishing a toehold with a stable of your ideal clients, bending over backward to satisfy their needs and thereby grow these client relationships together. The sales process for expansion or upsell opportunities with currently satisfied clients is considerably easier (and decidedly less expensive) than a path that involves finding new clients. You will be able to manage sales margin needs and, with careful consideration (and luck), more readily manage your churn.

You cannot wait for investors to find you and your pre-revenue company. Your endeavor will die while you're waiting for that "perfect deal" to come along. If you can manage organic growth, you may be able to demonstrate to investors what you can do *without* capital: with capital, you'll be able to goose the growth even faster.

## SALES CONSORTIUMS

When several otherwise unaffiliated people or companies get together to collaborate on a sales effort (for example, to bid on a major grant-funded project), they are often classified as a consortium. I have not had tremendous experience with consortiums, for a few reasons. First, at the beginning, there is great excitement with any such endeavor, but as time goes on, the honeymoon phase slips away, and the excitement wanes. Second, as much as everyone might want to see the larger group succeed, there is a selfish motive inherent to human survival—your commitment is first to the survival of your own company. Third, the more participants involved in the consortium, the higher the chance that interpersonal flare-ups may occur. Fourth, it is not possible that each member of the consortium can (or will) contribute precisely the same amount. It may be that one member will see others in a dim light, saying, "I contribute more to this than any of them," even if that is not true.

## PARTNERSHIPS/RESELLING

Partnerships are a somewhat different beast. If you can find another company that doesn't compete with yours directly, but with which you can complement their line of business in a seamless fashion, this can be a win/win for both of you. For example, value-added resellers (VARs) are integrators that look for products and services they can resell to their current roster of clients. It is not without effort: you will need to persuade the potential partner of the value of your service/offering and, on an ongoing basis, educate their salespeople on how to best position and present it and ensure that the profit margin of the resold offering is sufficient and that salespeople will meet their sales targets or goals when selling your product. None of this can be taken for granted. Try to avoid situations where partners/resellers demand exclusivity to resell (unless there is a significant up-front financial commitment that is made, plus a strict timeline to sunset that agreement).

Ideally, you'll want to focus on the "Four C's" of successful partnerships: customers, capacity, capability, and commitment. The ideal partner will have a set of customers that need your solution (and are within your ideal customer profile), the capacity to assign a dedicated stock-keeping unit (SKU) for the purpose of inventory management and ease-of-sales tracking, the capability to actually sell your offering (i.e., they are comfortable selling services if your offering demands it), and, finally, they are committed to unlocking their salespeople and customer base to you.

To that point, you cannot expect that when you sign a partnership deal that your work is done. Just as you would need to assist your own salespeople in building the sales process and articulating the product pitch script, you need to create a low-friction plan that the resellers' salespeople can follow to successfully resell your firm's offering.

I do not recommend working with direct competitors. Often larger companies will bid on contract work and then farm out the actual work to smaller firms (such as yourself) at a lower rate. Generally, in these cases, you are not able to disclose your own company's name or take credit for any work that is done. Ultimately, you are bolstering the larger company's reputation at the expense of your own. I recognize that from a business survival perspective, you might need to take the subcontracted gig just to sustain or maintain cash flow. If you must, take the gig, but otherwise, my recommendation is to be ruthless with your competition, give them no ground, share no secrets, and grant them no assistance.

## GROWTH THROUGH ACQUISITIONS

Even at an early stage, growing by acquisition is a possible strategy to realistically entertain. At a startup size, it is unlikely that you will find companies beyond the startup size available and interested in being acquired, but it is possible to acquire small "lone wolf" or "one/two person" shops to come on board. There are cases where you may be able to effect a power multiple—when combining two or more small companies, the output is greater than the sum of the independent parts. Assume that this process will be far from smooth: change is scary. There will be considerable adjustments needed across workplace culture and styles, and even seemingly simple items such as time zone adjustments for meetings can pose stress and confusion. Whether you like it or not, there will be months of the corporate "pecking order" being reshuffled and communicated multiple times. As the Chief Survival Officer, you'll need to keep on top of these items and address them before they become toxic.

## RUTHLESS OPTIMIZATION

This is a point where we must again address our earlier reference to economist David Ricardo's law of comparative advantage. In short, focus on that which you excel upon. In technology circles, this is often referred to as "homegrown" or do-it-yourself (DIY) efforts where it is considered common practice to roll your own code. Time is precious; don't write from scratch that which already exists and has been proven. Even if you could assemble the plumbing and HVAC in a house you're building, you might choose to let professionals do that work—you would certainly not build the components yourself. Similarly, when reviewing your business processes, there are components that might be best outsourced (even to "nearshore" or offshore resources where you can take advantage of labor and skills pricing arbitrage).

What is most important in the context of any of the accretive growth methods outlined in this chapter is that all parties are unified in their goals and are willing to commit to the success of the greater goals and performance of the company.

Growing your startup rarely takes a single path. Keep your eyes open for opportunities to collaborate, but do so only when it makes eminent sense, depending on your current obligations and capabilities. Do not give up your "secret sauce." Outsource and/or delegate noncore functionality to other trusted parties while exercising your core capabilities to their best use.

# CHAPTER 19

# Incubators and
# Accelerators

THEY MAY GO BY many names: Incubators. Accelerators. Innovation Hubs. In ideal form, they provide a nexus for founders, startups, business coaches and advisors, and on occasion, investors. The concept behind them all is that on a regular basis, several startups huddle together in a cohort to be advised on business topics (including some of what I have discussed in this book). Often these organizations house entrepreneurs-in-residence (EIRs)— business executives and former founders who have often sold or exited their startups and wish to keep engaged in the community.

The most famous is undoubtedly Y Combinator: the creator of the financial instrument called a "SAFE," which stands for "simple agreement for future equity," one of the most oft-used financial instruments for startups raising money. In certain pockets of the institutional investor community, there can be a halo effect associated with having been accepted into one of the top-flight startup accelerators, and that halo effect can win you clients, media attention, and further funding.

There are thousands of smaller business accelerators in the world; most are grouped by geography, nationality, or vertical (such as technology or life sciences). At their best, they help founders make connections and build their networks. They provide hands-on training and tools from a roster of EIRs. This training could include strategies for sales and marketing, scaling, and fundraising and can often help propel participants forward: truly accelerating their startup journey.

However, your mileage may vary. I would recommend that you do the research first to see if an accelerator is for you. Reach out through your own network and contact founders from startups that were in earlier cohorts. Ask the tough questions regarding the value of the program. You should recognize that there may be a significant time commitment on your behalf if you are accepted, and your participation may divert attention from your primary goal, which is to enable your company to survive and thrive.

Note that many accelerators are funded by taking early equity positions in the startups that they support. Generally, you should expect that accelerators that take equity positions will expect to acquire 5 to 10 percent of your company in exchange for providing mentorship, training, introductions, and funding. Here are typical examples of what equity positions several accelerators take once your startup has been accepted:

- Y Combinator: $125,000 USD for a 7 percent stake, $375,000 USD in an uncapped SAFE
- Techstars: $120,000 USD for a 6 percent stake
- 500 Startups: $150,000 USD for a 6 percent stake

You may note significant concerns with accelerators—the most obvious being that they can take a significant equity position in your company. Are you sure that you want to give up such a large amount so early? One recent example of how that might be especially problematic is the example of a US-based accelerator filing for bankruptcy while simultaneously recruiting more startups to join a new cohort under a newly-incorporated entity's name. You might not expect accelerators to go out of business, but if they do, you might find that your own startup's equity/warrants now belong to one or more of their creditors. Beware. Obtain excellent independent advice before signing *anything*.

In a somewhat similar vein, you should be alert to the fact that some early Series A investors don't see the value that accelerators offer a startup. These investors chafe at the thought of investing in startups that have already ceded a piece of the startup to an accelerator.

## ATTENDING THE LOCAL INNOVATION CENTER

*I had received an invitation to attend the grand opening of an innovation center in my hometown. I arrived; the parking lot was packed! Local dignitaries, politicians, and business leaders were all basking in the milieu: a beautiful new space for entrepreneurs to launch their endeavors. Government money had been spent to update an old building, completely remodeled with open space and small breakout offices and conference rooms and state-of-the-art Ethernet cabling throughout. I munched on cheese and crackers, had a little white wine, and later met and spoke with a few people. After about an hour, I took my leave. A few weeks later, I decided to stop by on a Saturday afternoon. No cars. No activity. No grinding. This was a marked difference to the grand opening. It is comparatively easy to start something rather than invest in ongoing care and maintenance, even when it is done with the very best of intentions.*

When it comes to accelerators, review the backgrounds of the current slate of mentors and EIRs. If there is someone who has specific experience from which you believe you could benefit, make a solid effort to get on their schedule. Don't expect them to chase you. Also, carefully vet these advisors; I have found that some are what I call "unmarried marriage counselors" (with little actual hands-on experience) and are simply looking to sell their services. If you have any contacts within the early-stage investor community or you know business leaders who have been through these programs in the recent past, you might want to seek their opinions before making a final decision on joining an accelerator.

Merely getting into an accelerator program is no different than being accepted into college: you need to be coachable, and you will need to put the time and effort in to get meaningful results. You should recognize that there will likely be a significant time commitment on your behalf if you are accepted.

Once accepted, be aware of "groupthink" among your cohort. I have found that some startup founders get addicted to the accelerator life and collect badges of that life as though they are Pokémon cards. Don't let them distract you from your true mission: your startup's survival and commercial success. Take the advice you hear from people associated with the accelerator with a fist-sized grain of salt, always test hypotheses, make connections, and be sure to use the resources that are made available to you. Ideally you will be able to find fellow founders, mentors, and other people who inspire you to keep moving forward on your commitment to succeed.

## INSIDE THE ROGERS CYBERSECURITY CATALYST

*I have had the great fortune to be an EIR for the Rogers Cybersecurity Catalyst at Toronto Metropolitan University since early 2021. It featured what I believe to be the essential components truly required for success: a stellar curriculum for founders, a deep bench of capable and experienced EIRs, and excellent connections into both the corporate and investment communities. If you're looking for guidance and support (outside of the cybersecurity-specific field), I would suggest looking for a well-tenured accelerator with a similar flywheel of capabilities and features.*

What we've seen in this chapter is that accelerators can help startups build their networks, gain traction, and shine a light on a startup's blind spots. But none of this is guaranteed; you will need to do your own research first to see if the commitment (time, opportunity cost, and equity) is worth your effort and won't distract you from your primary commitment: your startup.

# CHAPTER 20

# Funding

I F THE GOAL FOR your technology company is significant growth, at some point, you will undoubtedly require capital.

In the early days, you shouldn't be surprised if you'll need to fund your startup by yourself (or from what might be called "bootstrapping"). I am loath to recommend reaching out to members of your closest network to help fund your incredibly risky venture (what is colloquially called a "friends and family" round) unless they recognize that the chances of them completely losing their investment in you are overwhelming. There are also second-order concerns that can arise. As a specific example, your siblings may want to know why they haven't been extended the same courtesy. This can make holiday gatherings uncomfortable; you should expect that every year you will be asked, "So, what's going on with my money?" The timeline of a founder's financial success is rarely less than ten years from inception—this firmly categorizes this investment as highly risky, illiquid, and long term.

Statistically speaking, if you're a first-time founder without connections, the odds of you raising capital for your idea alone (pre-revenue) are exceedingly small. As a result, some model of self-funding is realistically the most appropriate and available way to fund your first startup.

Unfortunately, because your own capital is likely quite limited, your potential is restrained, and so, at best, you can obtain organic growth (as opposed to acquisition-style growth) through self-funding.

*At the start of eSentire, we didn't raise any outside money, even from friends or family. Perhaps it is a personality quirk of mine; I didn't want to be beholden to anyone else. I didn't want family members to ask me, "What's happening with my money?" on holidays or at family events. If we were to fail, I didn't want to bring anyone down along with me.*

There's nothing wrong with organic growth; you can build a fantastic lifestyle business and grow at a reasonable and manageable rate over time. Before you decide to raise outside capital, you need to consider your desired outcomes. If you're comfortable running a boutique company or don't want to give up any portion of the business to anyone else (or want to answer to anyone else), stop thinking about raising capital and just execute. However, raising money may help to de-risk your own investment.

Before raising capital, you need to consider alternative methods to finance your startup. If your offering is a product, carefully consider a services option (for example, one with MRR) and/or a consulting arm. Recognize that in the future, revenue that comes from an adjacent vector will be treated by interested investors as separate revenue streams, each of which might get a different valuation multiple. While there are notable exceptions, in general, new product offerings can claim a higher valuation multiple than recurring services, which in turn can claim a higher valuation multiple than pure hourly consulting. There may also be government assistance (grants, tax credits, or in-kind options) available to you.

If you have already pursued all manner of strategies of increasing your revenue on your own and still have decided that you want to grow faster than can be achieved organically, you'll likely need external funding.

Let's first set the stage for the level of external funding you're most likely to discuss at the early stage.

**Pre-seed Funding**: Obtain enough capital to validate the product-solution fit and build a prototype.

**Seed Funding**: Obtain enough capital to identify product/market fit, move the offering out of beta, and determine what go-to-market approaches work to enable the company to scale.

**Series A Funding**: Obtain enough capital to validate the business model, scale the company, and develop a repeatable go-to-market motion (i.e., as a flywheel that "makes money while you sleep").

There are pros and cons to venture funding. Some pros may include the potential for faster growth through the use of proceeds, and getting assistance from your backers (whether it be advice or connections/introductions) in addition to the capital raised (sometimes known as "smart money"). The cons may include pressures you had not yet experienced, including pressure to grow at a faster rate, pressure to exit the business, and conceivably further rigor regarding oversight and governance.

If you've truly set your heart on it, do not get carried away with paroxysms of joy at the thought of a capital raise. So often I have heard founders brag about a particular funding round as in "We just closed a 250K round!" Or "So-and-so just closed a $1.2 million raise!" Do not confuse raising money with commercial success. Unfortunately, self-broadcasting by founders (particularly on social media) reinforces this confusion. There is nothing wrong with making an announcement regarding a successful fund raise but use it as a marketing/public relations opportunity rather than bragging for the sake of bragging.

I want to point out a few items:

First, the investors have not brought you money without an expectation of a substantial future payoff, and the clock has started to tick.

Second, I can guarantee that the money raised will not last as long as you think it will.

Third, you should expect that investors may ask for reporting and accountability, and possibly adherence to certain principles consistent with their investment hypothesis. These could include principles related to ethics, ESG, or selling into specific customer segments or launching specific lines of business.

Fourth, the funding announcement that's ultimately released, having been vetted by investors and public relations, never shows the deep specifics of the deal—you should assume that only the best facets of the deal have been polished, emphasized, and released.

*I want to explicitly state that I'm not a fan of what I have defined as the entrepreneur-tainment oeuvre, be it Shark Tank or Dragons' Den or so on. It might make for fun television, but it is more than unrealistic so you shouldn't expect that when you start pitching potential investors, any of it will follow the TV-style scripts. First, I believe TV pitch shows vastly minimize the time that's spent during the entire process, and in particular, the due diligence effort behind the scenes. As well, they don't generally show what firms ultimately failed (or exited) from the due diligence and investment even if they may have appeared to have "won" on the episode. Just because you watched nineteen seasons of Grey's Anatomy doesn't mean that you know what it is like to work in a hospital. Having said that, I will say that there are aspects of these shows that are plausible. The more plausible aspects focus on questions about the startup's numbers ("What are the annual sales?" "How much are you asking to raise?" "For what percentage of the company?" "What are your profit margins?").*

How can you determine what potential investors are looking for and how can you make your company look even more attractive to them?

Generally, investors don't want to fund a mere idea. Ideas are easy; operational execution of that idea to deliver profit is exceptionally difficult. Any given investor will have the opportunity to look at literally several hundreds (if not well into the thousands) of companies every year, and any single wholly unproven idea may be a difficult investment to make, especially when myriad other companies may already have working prototypes and/or sales to provide supporting evidence of product-market fit. It is said that pitching an idea for possible investment before the offering exists is called "raising on the dream." You might be able to do this *once* in the life of a given company. If you're successful, the next funding round will demand that you "raise on the data."

## THE FIRST MILLION IS THE
## MOST DIFFICULT

*Though the potential payoff could be very high, investing in an early-stage company that is under $1 million USD in annual revenues is very risky—especially when the startup is headed by a first-time founder. One million USD in revenue seems to be a specific pivot point where suddenly your startup is* *considerably more interesting to investors. This is especially so if this revenue is expected to recur in some form.*

*If you have achieved an annualized recurring revenue of one million dollars, you have proven a few things: First, you have demonstrated that your offering meets a need in the market. Second, you have demonstrated that you've achieved some traction and some product market fit. Third, you now have some good data regarding the sales process and approach. You can now perform better analysis on target markets and price elasticity. Fourth, you may have some valuable metrics regarding contract renewals.*

*The milestone of reaching the $1 million USD milestone in recurring revenues begins to de-risk any potential investment an early-stage investor may choose to make.*

*You might find that given the economic climate that early-stage investors might be more comfortable with you meeting a $2 million USD milestone. Some investors view $1 million USD as evidence that you have sold well within your own network but $2 million USD demonstrates that you have extended your market beyond it.*

*There are always exceptions to these rules, especially if you find yourself in a particularly frothy category (e.g., GenAI in late 2023/early 2024).*

Each investment group with which you may meet has its own personality and characteristics, and while they're looking to invest in you, it is critical that you examine them as well. Investing is a partnership with the need for flexibility and compatibility. Each investor group will have a "sweet spot" of funding, where they have historically been most comfortable. These characteristics will include their investment thesis, favored verticals, typical deal size, and investment horizon. You may hear terms such as "smart money," which may refer to their expertise or knowledge within a particular type of business or within a specific vertical.

This is as good a time as any to underscore that there are several broad categories of investors. These categories aren't necessarily carved in stone; there are large growth equity funds that host accelerators for small startups in need of seed funding, but in general, what follows are the broad categories of investors you will come across.

In the early stages, there are angels or so-called seed funds. They might include accelerator groups, formal family offices, or high-net-worth (HNW) investors, many of whom might have previously trod the very road you're on. Many angels I have met are former founders who successfully exited their businesses but want to keep engaged in the environment and encourage the next generation of founders, using their own money to fund startups. This is likely the group in which you will be searching for your first outside investment money.

Next are a broad group of venture capital firms (colloquially known as VCs). They generally follow seed and angel rounds up with Series A through successive rounds such as Series B, C, and D.

The final broad category of investors consists of growth equity through to private equity (PE) groups. I am including here large investor groups such as pension funds. They usually fund larger companies; either private companies headed to the public market (IPO) or public firms that are looking to become privately held again.

There may be significant overlap among adjacent categories; they may vary in size and in assets under management (AUM). Keep in mind that you will likely be talking to seed investors or angels or the smallest of VCs at your startup size unless the larger firms have specific groups that cater to early investments.

On that point, let's dig deeper into the angel/early-stage seed investor realm.

Angels are typically HNW individuals who have decided to try their hand at investing in early-stage companies for any number of reasons. Some want to balance their portfolios by extending their exposure to riskier opportunities (and if they're lucky, to a corresponding outsized return), while others want to participate and "give back" to founders of companies they find interesting. There is often overlap in their goals. Some are more serious than others: "cocktail investing" is on the less serious side of the spectrum, while on the more serious side of the spectrum you may find more formal family funds or full-time investors interested. You may find these angels come from a wide variety of backgrounds: dentists, executives, or retired founders looking for the next "game" to play.

Angels rarely source individual deals; they are more often exposed to deal flow through angel groups. Angel groups solicit individual investors to become members; often in turn for membership fees, they source and vet interesting startups for organized pitch events. Some angel groups focus on particular verticals (such as life sciences, or SaaS tech) while others take a broader approach (for example, looking at new ventures locally). Rarely would any single angel within a group choose to entirely fund your raise; it is more likely that if they were interested in participating, other angels would gain interest and follow their lead. The "fear-of-missing-out" (or "FOMO") does not only occur within angel groups; we will discuss this further during the final stages of the raise process ("make a market").

Founders usually reach out to angel groups in order to present at pitch meetings. The angel group staff will vet all candidates to identify which seem to be the most promising. If you are not accepted, don't take it personally; the staff are searching for the startups they feel might be most interesting to their specific type of investors.

If accepted to present at an angel pitch event, you will typically be given fifteen minutes to introduce your company, the offering, use of proceeds, and finally, the "ask" (how much you are looking to raise through what investment vehicle), followed by a Q&A session. This portion closely resembles the entrepreneur-tainment television shows you see. However, don't expect to get an answer immediately. After the pitch day, the assembled investors are asked if they are interested in pursuing further investigation. If there is interest, generally one investor volunteers (or is chosen) to lead the due diligence. At this point, due diligence may take weeks and ultimately might not lead to any deal.

One particularly beneficial aspect of pitching to angel groups is that they can help streamline or minimize the paperwork behind investing. If you are lucky enough to connect with an angel group that specializes in your category (e.g., technology,) you might find that a combination of angels can each contribute small checks (say, as low as $5K USD) that can aggregate up to the amount you're looking to raise, while also extending your network and visibility through to their networks. It can be a very good look to have well-known angels participating in early rounds, adding value by association well beyond the face value of the check size.

In a similar vein, entities such as AngelList or Sydecar can offer founders an easier path to fundraising by offering services to either roll up smaller checks and/or to make the necessary collection and administration of these checks to be both far easier and cheaper than if it were managed by a law firm.

## WHAT DO ANGELS ULTIMATELY WANT?

*I find that it is infinitely valuable during any negotiation (including sales or investment) to assess the viewpoint of the person on the other side of the table—to walk a mile in their shoes. To that point, what do angels want?*

*Aside from some altruistic social benefits discussed a few paragraphs ago: to make outsized returns on their own post-tax money. So how can angel investors make money?*

*In theory, it is very simple. Due to the inherent riskiness of early investment, angel investors expect that only one investment in 5 (or 10) pays off. A theoretical angel portfolio that has 10 investments in their portfolio (to be considered a marked success) may turn out as follows: Five will completely crater, one will return most of the money invested, two will return either all of the money invested or a healthy multiple (e.g., a two to five times return), and the one remaining will be a rocket (e.g., 10–100 times return).*

*I want to start by explicitly stating that the rough math here to follow is simplified and as such is not quite accurate because VCs typically buy existing shares (from earlier tranches) at a 10–25 percent discount. So, for the sake of keeping the math simple, let's temporarily ignore this discount.*

*Imagine an angel invests in a SaaS startup at a $5 million USD valuation. Let's say that the startup's ARR is $500K and their enterprise valuation was 10x ARR.*

*ARR = $500K*

*Multiple = 10x*

*Enterprise valuation: $500K * 10 = $5M*

*Let's say that this SaaS startup uses the investment very efficiently and performs very well from a sales perspective, and the ARR turns into $5 million USD in two years. If the multiple (10x) remains the same, $50 million USD would be the new enterprise valuation:*

> *ARR = $5M*
> *Multiple = 10x*
> *Enterprise valuation: $5M \* 10 = $50M*

*The startup's success then catches the eye of several VCs; one makes an offer that is accepted, and as a result, they buy the angel's shares. The angel will make a nominal 10x return on their investment (keeping in mind the discount caveat mentioned earlier).*

*However, if global macro conditions change, there can be a direct negative impact. Early 2023 is a perfect example: the global economy wobbled and sharply increased interest rates have permeated strategy in the investment world. All investors (including angels) are looking for better deals, and valuation multiples have also decreased.*

*Let's look at a different two-year outcome:*

*Let's say that again, this SaaS startup uses the investment very efficiently and performs very well from a sales perspective, and the ARR becomes $5M in two years. However, due to underlying macro conditions, the multiple moves from 10x to 5x, $25m would be the new enterprise valuation:*

> *ARR = $5M*
> *Multiple = 5x*
> *Enterprise valuation: $5M \* 5 = $25M*

*To extend the previous example: the startup's success catches the eye of several VCs; one makes an offer that is accepted, and as a result they buy the angel's shares. However, due to the reduction multiple, the angel will make a nominal 5x return on their investment (again, ignoring a 10–25 percent discount for the sake of keeping the math simple). The valuation multiple declined faster than the revenue increased.*

*But luckily, the reverse is also true. If an angel invests in a SaaS startup at a 5x revenue multiple, and after two years, it can take advantage of improved global macro conditions when the valuation multiple has bounced back to 10x. The angel investor in this example would then make a nominal 20x return on their investment.*

*Angels hope that all of their investments can yield outsized returns, but as I've stated explicitly several times earlier, startups are by their very nature very risky.*

*Given this information, how can you catch an angel's attention? They want you to show them how your startup will be the one in ten that yields an outsized return. I suggest that you pitch to angels with the same rigor you would employ as though you were pitching to larger investment players.*

## EARLY-STAGE FINANCIAL MODELLING

*You should accept the fact that the vast majority of early-stage financial models are practically worthless; they are barely more than guesstimation at this point. Investors recognize this.*

*Despite this, keep in mind that your financial models should back up your pitch deck by using data, for example: "We are currently at this place; if we allocate funds as we have stated to specific areas of our business and focus on same, we believe we can achieve this outcome."*

*There are two primary areas of focus that early-stage investors want to see in your early-stage financial model:*

*First, they want to see a cost-and-burn structure to discover how you plan to maximize your runway with the capital influx. You may not yet have product-market-fit (PMF); will you have sufficient runway to find it?*

*Second, when costs and burn are detailed, what assumptions do you make regarding revenue generation—not necessarily how much revenue is being generated, but what are your sources of interested clients and deal flow? While revenue is unknown, costs and burn are generally well known.*

*This is what they want to see.*

Seasoned investors will minimally evaluate a potential investment in a company on five characteristics:

- The Team

  - Specifically, they will be digging deep into your team's background, dynamics, cohesion, and how well-spoken and thoughtful they are

- The Offering

  - Specifically, what pain points are being solved? Can it be considered mission-critical? Can you calculate the ROI? Is there a moat against competitors? Will it be difficult to replicate by new or existing competitors? Will said moat get deeper as the company grows and matures (e.g., increasing the body of work, through data gathered, machine-learning models, proprietary datasets)? What is the vision for the product offering? What is on the roadmap?

- The Numbers (Sales)

  - Is there an efficient, robust and thoughtful business model? Do you have evidence/proof points from paying customers? Is there price elasticity? Are you potentially leaving money on the table?

- The Customers

  - What do customers say about your product? Are they rabid fans? Do they or will they act as vocal advocates on your behalf? Do they refer you to other customers? Will they renew once their contract term is completed? If you are pre-revenue, are there potential customers that claim that they \*would\* pay for this solution once available?

- The Market

  - Finally, what are the market dynamics? How do global economic conditions affect the business model? Who are your competitors? Are there regulations surrounding your business model (including but not merely relating to data collected, used, and stored)? What trends do you see in the marketplace?

Ultimately, the best (and smartest) early-stage investors want to work with entrepreneurs who have both a clear vision and can clearly articulate their offering's differentiation.

Early-stage investors (including angels) are more likely to recognize that you may not have the track record or metrics (especially if you're pre-revenue) demanded by more seasoned investors. They are more likely to focus on their perceptions of the team and the proposed offering.

In any case, as they perform deeper due diligence, all investors will have more specific questions that may expand to include the following:

- How well does your company fit in with their investment thesis and existing family of investments?
- Do you have a big vision that will help them achieve their outsized investment goals?

- Is the market in which you're selling growing faster than others?
- Do you have a particularly interesting and different insight within your space that your competition hasn't discovered yet?
- Can you describe how you would scale your company?
- Do you have a moat around your company that would support or enhance your scaling efforts?
- How successful have the members of the team been in the past?
- What are their duties and what is their coverage/overlap?
- Have they worked together previously?
- What is their commitment to this startup?
- Does the offering fit a need in the market?
- How does the offering compare to that of the competition?
- What does your go-to-market strategy look like? Has it been successful to date?
- What is on the product runway?
- What are your current revenue numbers (or are they pre-revenue)?
- What does your cash flow look like?
- How many clients do you have?
- How do you source lead generation?
- What is the average revenue from each client?
- Have you had clients renew their contracts? What is your annual churn?
- How much time do you have until your current funding is exhausted? This is colloquially referred to as your "runway."
- In what markets have you enjoyed the most success?
- What are the plans for the use of proceeds from this funding raise? What would create the biggest positive impact on sales?

And so many, many more questions.

In short, they would like to see a sensible and robust business model and details regarding how you will judiciously use the capital raised to grow the business and make both you and them wildly successful.

They will also want to know the details regarding what percentage of the company you're willing to sell them. I have found that during the early stages, no single investor will want to take more than 15–20 percent of the company. The intention of the seed round is to prove out an early prototype of the company and see if it can survive in the cutthroat business environment. By only taking a minority position in the company, they are looking to support your motion forward and not disincentivizing you from that progress.

When you're pitching, I recommend that you have appropriate revenue metrics prepared and ready to answer quickly (as appropriate to your business, recognizing that some metrics may not apply). Note that many of these revenue metrics are those mentioned earlier in the sales and sales metrics portions of this book. These include the following:

- Monthly recurring revenue (MRR)—the monthly total of recurring revenue
- Annualized recurring revenue (ARR)—recurring revenue on an annual basis
- Committed annual recurring revenue (CARR)
- Average revenue per account (ARPA)
- Gross profit
- Total contract value (TCV)
- Annual contract value (ACV)
- Customer lifetime value (LTV)
- Deferred revenue
- Billings
- Customer acquisition cost (CAC)

- Customer acquisition cost payback period (e.g., are they less than 12 months?)
- LTV:CAC ratio (are they at least 3:1?)
- Client concentration risk (e.g., is there one client that contributes the lion's share of revenue? Are your clients concentrated in one specific vertical or geopgraphy?)
- Daily active users (DAU)
- Monthly active users (MAU)
- Number of logins
- Activation rate
- Month-on-month (MoM) growth rate
- Compounded monthly growth rate (CMGR)
- Monthly churn rate
- Gross retention
- Gross churn rate
- Growth rate
- Net churn
- Burn rate

Bear in mind this caveat: at a pre-seed/angel round, you might not have gathered enough data to provide any reasonable values to these metrics. Find out what are the appropriate "golden metrics" for YOUR company and vertical and focus on generating those data.

Are you overwhelmed yet? Don't worry; these are the kinds of metrics you will commit to heart and commit to love on your startup journey. Think of it as a market test of your own commitment. If you don't care enough about knowing why these metrics are important to measure, then maybe you're not cut out for the commitment required.

## EARLY-STAGE INVESTOR RED FLAGS

In general, early-stage or angel investors may not be as sophisticated as those you may find in later-stage funds. There are a few red flags/warning signs that you may encounter from angels:

1. You are their first angel investment.
2. They might tell you that you shouldn't be paying yourself at this early stage.
3. They might "soft commit" to an investment, but it is contingent on an exit event from another one of their investments.
4. They might demand a wide variety of metrics (including those just listed above) for which you don't have sufficient data.
5. They demand liquidation preferences and/or anti-dilution clauses.
6. They ask for detailed "exit plans" before you've really hit your stride.
7. Working through a prolonged due diligence process for a relatively small investment (e.g., less than $100K).
8. Demanding a board seat for a relatively small investment.
9. Taking multiple meetings but never giving feedback (e.g., prolonging the process unnecessarily).
10. Demanding excessive face time/micro-management: weekly check-ins, after-hours texts/calls, demanding strategy shifts (contingent on investment).
11. Simply being a jerk. Haughty, rude, arrogant.

Don't be steamrolled by early-stage investors making outrageous demands. They can be valuable partners in your journey, but you don't want to be overwhelmed by excessive demands on their part.

What Should You Be Asking Investors?

Just as you will be asked questions, it's only fair that you qualify investors themselves. It's essential that you prepare for any conversation by researching angels/VCs in advance. Investors generally have a fairly well-defined 4-tuple of thesis:check size:stage:personality and it's critical that this mesh well with your firm and yourself.

Specific questions that you should ask during the early meetings might include:

- What is your investment thesis?
- Do you lead or follow investments?
- What is your typical check size?
- What is the stage when you normally invest, and what are the criteria for investments you make? These could include ARR, the presence of paying clients, clear proof of PMF, specific geographies or verticals.
- Do you participate in future rounds?
- What markets and/or verticals do you typically invest in?
- Are you a specialist fund (e.g., fintech, climate tech, deep tech) or a generalist (investing in any startup of a certain stage and/or broad market)?
- What fund are you investing from? How much dry powder do you have left in this specific fund?
- When did you raise this fund? Note that funds are generally more likely to invest near the beginning of a new fund then when at the end of a fund's lifecycle (where they are undoubtedly more cautious and thoughtful of the fit of the company into their overall portfolio).
- What is your "special sauce," your differentiators and value-add to this relationship?

Some of this information is available publicly or through sites such as Crunchbase. Do your research before you have a meeting, go in prepared with what you have discovered and see if the answers they give agree with what is detailed online.

While many angels work as solo practitioners, it is important to get a sense as to what corporate structures exist in larger firms. To wit: expanding beyond angels and other early-stage investors, the typical staff hierarchy within a VC firm is (ignoring subcategories of specialty VCs):

- Partners
- Principals
- Associates
- Analysts

Just because there is an established hierarchy, there's no need to disparage interactions with any "lesser" employees. You must recognize that each group has its duties and responsibilities essential to the functioning of the firm. In fact, one of the softer evaluation techniques used by VC and angel group leaders is how you interact with all levels of an organization, including the person whom you meet at the reception desk.

Consider that Venture Capital works as an apprenticeship model. Partners ultimately decide what deals are funded (during investment meetings). Principals should be considered 'Partners-In-Training', doing much of the heavy lifting, including reaching out to subject matter experts (SMEs) that can help vet companies during due diligence. Associates will make (or take) hundreds of introductory calls every year to fill a deal flow funnel. Just because they are taking your call doesn't mean their fund is actively investing. Associates are generally given a quota of companies to which they are to reach out each quarter. Do not assume that they are necessarily interested—they might just be filling their quota. You might also need to realize that associates may be just doing raw research, with no intent to invest in you whatsoever. They may have an interest in a competitor of yours and are just trying to see what information they can milk out of you. They may have already invested in a competitor (a current portfolio company of theirs) or are in the process of performing their due diligence for that competitor!

In addition to the questions listed earlier that you should ask potential VC's, you should take the opportunity to investigate their process themselves. These questions could include:

- How is the decision about this potential deal to be made?
- What does the overall diligence process look like?
- What should I (as the entrepreneur/founder) expect as the next steps in both process and timing?
- Who will lead the deal? The person to which you're currently speaking or someone more senior?

If their intent is legitimate, and if there is something of interest that an associate discovers during their initial meeting with you, they may begin to create an investment case for further review. This investment case will further be built out by analysts who may do the grunt work for associates (including detailing and expanding upon the initial due diligence as discovered earlier in your discussion or online).

You need to realize a few things: due to the process I've detailed, you will undoubtedly need to tell your story several times, even to the same VC firm. If you're lucky, it is an ever-expanding audience within this investment team, so consider that a good sign. Understandably, this process may take a significant amount of time, even over several pitches. If you're made impatient by this process, stop trying to raise money and just build your company through organic means. The capital raise process, like almost everything else that leads to success, will take considerably longer than you expect.

Ultimately, associates at a VC firm will refer vetted investment candidates up to principals and partners during weekly status meetings, and eventually, if there is interest, this should lead to a scheduled investment meeting where all members of the firm (plus any subject matter experts who act as advisors) will be in attendance. After this meeting, the various parties will decide if there is interest in moving ahead with the investment. You should be prepared for this investment meeting as you should expect at this point to be grilled about every single facet of your company and its future plans.

As associates are the "thin edge of the wedge," if you believe that at some point in the future you be interested in raising capital, it is important that early on you build relationships with them (well before you need to raise). I recommend that you meet with them regularly (e.g., during conferences), keep them in the loop regarding your progress. Consider this your early "relationship building" phase.

To this point, it is essential that you create a target list of potential investors and gradually get to know them, to see if they are a fit with you!

If you wish to "make a market" (where a number of investors are interested in your company and are willing to compete to participate), it is essential that you court this pool of potential investors and create an environment where they are regularly reminded of your firm's current situation and trajectory. If you can create a reasonable and itchy level of FOMO to invest, it can be helpful when you eventually go to market. It is critical while you're in the process of building FOMO to be reasonable, even understated and gradually turn up the heat. Don't overstate your business' progress, including exaggerating pipeline, ARR, and/or namedropping clients.

Most importantly, never lie about the stage you are in with other VC's. Don't claim that a term sheet is "on its way" if that is not actually the case.

As a Chief Survival Officer, it is critical that you are both persistent and patient should you choose to proceed with raising capital. Succeeding with VC's is definitely a numbers game and the game can be cracked with enough persistence.

*There are many different vehicles for investment rounds; to describe them all is well outside the scope of this book. However, I do recommend two excellent and substantial resources: the book* Venture Deals *(by Brad Field and Jason Mendelson) and FeelTheBoot.com (Lance Cottrell's passion project). Early on, you will quite likely be using a version of the Y Combinator's SAFE vehicle. This well-established route is generally preferred by founders due to its simplicity, though you will find that many seed/early investors have somewhat soured on them since their early days and with good reason. First, SAFEs have no maturity date so that the instrument can sit on the company's books indefinitely without a mechanism to monetize or exit. If the company never achieves a priced round, qualified financing, or a sale, then the investor may never receive a return on their investment. Second, if the company is liquidated, there may be no recourse for the SAFE investor as they do not have the same rights that either a common or preferred shareholder would have (including voting or the ability to claim a breach of contract). A founder might be able to raise multiple rounds through successive SAFEs and never raise a priced round, and there is little recourse to the SAFE investor outside of moral suasion. A complicated series of SAFEs that are inconsistent (note: there are more than one flavor of SAFE in existence) may be looked upon by an investor pricing a formal round as being too complicated to deal with. In short, while they don't require a lot of paperwork, SAFEs may not be very safe for the founder. Know your instrument.*[1]

## PERHAPS YOUR STARTUP IS "UNINVESTABLE"

Consider for a moment that despite all the excitement of startup conferences, accelerators, and flashy media stories talking about startups raising money that you find yourself, after meeting with any number of angels and/or VCs, you've had absolutely no success. Ask yourself, "why?"

Perhaps your startup (at least at this present time) is simply uninvestable. There are many possible reasons or explanations for this.

Consider that the terms for investment could not be mutually attractive to both the founder and investor. We can't ignore external influences. The state of global macroeconomic decline, the sudden jump in interest rates, and the serious retraction of the public markets in late 2022 through 2023 certainly weigh on investor appetites. There's not much you can do about this than trim your sails and survive. What *is* under your control?

The 5-tuple of team/offering/numbers/customers/market is what sits at the core of investor disinterest. If the team is weak, the offering is uninteresting, and there is no data suggesting an impressive return. Why would anyone choose to commit capital to this venture?

---

1   As you can undoubtedly infer, there are trade-offs and pitfalls for every investment vehicle including SAFEs, and it is important that you, as a founder, at least have a broad understanding of them and their most effective uses. One of the best descriptions of the pros and cons of SAFEs may be found at https://www.dlapiper.com/en/insights/publications/2020/07/demystifying-safes

So much of the fundraising efforts involve creating a story that excites an investor. You truly need to put yourself into the investor's shoes and find messaging that motivates them. Nobody said that it was going to be easy.

Your team might just be uninspiring. You might be uncomfortable speaking to people. Identify your strengths and focus on them. Perhaps work with others to improve your public speaking (for example, join a local Toastmaster's club). Hone your pitch, and be ready for difficult questions with preparation.

Or the offering might not resonate with the investor groups. Perhaps it's too niche or too abstract. Perhaps the investor has a current investment that is too similar, and they're conflicted (make sure you check their existing portfolio company list before pitching). Perhaps there's simply too much competition in this space already. Perhaps the technology is past its prime or its "hype cycle." Equally difficult: it might be too early! Is there a better way to present it to an outsider? You might be too close to view it with a critical eye that only a dispassionate outsider has.

Your numbers (i.e., the finances) are one of the best quantitative indicators of possible future success and give investors the most leverage to grind down the valuation (if they wish). Similarly, the existing capitalization table (colloquially referred to as the "cap table") may give indications of future problems. Let's dig into this for a bit because even when you're raising money, you should consider what impact it could have on your cap table (and on future funding rounds).

The cap table details existing equity arrangements (i.e., "who owns what") across possible tranches of investment. A messy cap table can be a serious red flag to investors. These messy elements could include the following:

Founders with less than 80 percent (combined) of the company before a seed round. Dilution upon subsequent rounds is guaranteed (and during a "down round," it is even more painful). If founders already start off at a disadvantage, they may soon find themselves diluted so far that there is scant remaining incentive to remain because the eventual payoff is not worth the effort.

Founders that have been heavily diluted by a previous lead investor (who holds too much control) and can't (or won't) provide necessary follow-on capital may find themselves hamstrung and unable to scale. The previous lead investor may be able to block all subsequent capital raises. Similarly, if the previous lead investor has clauses in effect (anti-dilutionary language), then this can be a significant disincentive for a new investor to join.

"Dead equity" refers to equity given to previous founders (or entities such as research universities) that own more than 10 percent (combined) of the company. Founders or entities that no longer contribute to the company (either in an active role or through capital commitment) are a drag on incentivization. Similarly, non-capital participating organizations, advisors, or angels who appear on the cap table due to providing a service in the past may often hold significant equity allocations without the company-protective guardrails of vesting schedules or performance hurdles.

Finally, a cap table with too many small investors may be seen as too much of a problem to be worth the trouble to a new investor. Often subsequent investors will demand that the cap table be "cleaned up" with earlier investors bought out to minimize future problems associated with voting rights.

Any single one or combination of the above may be cause for every single investor to politely thank you for their time and ask you to keep them informed, but decline.

Note that should an investor choose to decline, I recommend that you seek feedback from them regarding the specifics of why they passed. It is possible that they won't tell you, and it may very well be that what they do tell you will piercingly hurt like your first breakup, but you might learn a lot from this information (including how to pitch to the next set of investors). After receiving investor feedback, I beg of you: be gracious with thanks for the feedback. Do not argue with them as to why they are wrong and you are right. They have made up their mind; there is nothing further to be gained and they will remember you (negatively) in any future encounter should you meet again.

It is entirely possible that you haven't yet met the right investor.

What I've sought to show in this chapter is how funding—at the appropriate time and terms—can help your startup move forward, but a capital raise should not be the raison d'etre of your company. It is essential to understand the personality and intent of all those with whom you are growing your company through any funding vehicle. Recognize that the entire funding process is lengthy, and it's dependent on many different aspects, some of which are entirely out of your control. Any capital you may be fortunate to raise is not yours. It has been entrusted to you to make the best decisions for the company, to improve the outcomes of your investors, and to stay within the bounds of your fiduciary, ethical, and moral duties to all your shareholders.

# CHAPTER 21

# The Pitch Deck

Y OU WILL NEED TO put together a pitch deck to concisely describe the problem you're solving in the market, the size of the market, the strengths of your team, your runway, growth prospects, and, finally, to convey your big "ask." If you have never either assembled a pitch deck or pitched before, get advice. Go online and find examples. Put yourself in the investor's shoes: if you were an investor, what would you want to see before you put your hard-earned money into someone's dream?

As I've said, entire books have been written on assembling the "perfect" pitch deck. Here are a few small but critical points I want to emphasize since I repeatedly see people fail on them.

One: quickly get to the point and catch their attention. I have seen stats that say the typical pitch deck gets less than a few minutes of review at the first pass. If this is the case, you'd better quickly make an impact. Identify the problem and show how you solve it. Excite them.

Two: don't make it all about yourself personally. You aren't the most important component. Demonstrate how well your offering can solve a problem and show the investor how they're going to be able to make a significant profit from their early investment. Yes, you are an important component. The investor needs to believe in you that you'll stick to your goals and survive and thrive and that your personality will help grow the company and that they'll be able to work with you along the journey. Address the problem first and announce the team's bench strength near the end.

Three: don't inflate or fluff your logo page. The world of early-venture investing is a very small world; so, don't use client logos if you don't have their explicit permission to do so. I guarantee that any interested investor doing due diligence will work their network and find out whether your solution is actually being used and whatever other details can be obtained (i.e., was it a proof of concept or sandbox? what were the pricing details? were there favors called in to secure the job?). Prevarication of any kind in a pitch deck can sour any potential deal.

Four: don't inflate current revenue numbers. The truth is so important in every aspect of your journey but particularly here. Don't inflate your pipeline numbers. If you're early in your startup journey, it is likely that you don't have statistics to support projected growth. Don't say, for example, that the cybersecurity market is $3 trillion USD in total: that is meaningless to the current situation. Investors would ideally like to see actual "hockey stick growth"; they want to be sold on your vision of how their money will help to scale the business rapidly—the so-called 100x return. I have seen many five-year projections that are practically impossible; I don't believe that any investor truly believes in them because when so early in your journey, it is not possible to see that far into the future. It is better to put forward a sensible and defensible business model with reasonable assumptions where the investor can see the growth and profitability levers, and how you will make adjustments where necessary if things go better (or worse) than you have stated.

There's a term in business strategy referred to as a "big hairy audacious goal" (BHAG). Decide on your BHAG, and within your company explicitly identify it as such. We will discuss the BHAG in greater depth in the "Surviving Success" chapter.

Five: assume that once you release the pitch deck, it is available for public consumption, including to competitors. You could insist that investors sign non-disclosure agreements (NDAs) before taking a meeting, but you will likely find it severely limits your audience (as few will sign). At this early stage, your idea is probably not that distinctive or unique. In any case, ideas are plentiful. Repeatable successful execution is what matters more.

Six: use of proceeds should focus on company growth. This typically means that the majority of the raise should go toward sales and marketing efforts. This can be an unpopular point. It is truly a rare investor who wants you to use their money to investigate new ideas. They would prefer an offering that has had some limited success but would be valuable to a larger audience (say, in different verticals, locations, or adjacent markets). Your idea might be very interesting to you, but in my experience, investors don't want to pay for your investigatory experimental prototypes. They want you to use their money to act as the catalyst for massive growth (and payoff). They don't want you to use their money to pay off earlier loans, and unless they're looking to clean up an existing cap table, they likely don't want to pay off earlier investors.

My personal preference is to hold back on seeking external investment until you're totally ready to spring forward and execute in a growth manner. Do not find yourself in a situation where you have less than a year's runway to start a capital raise process; nearing the precipice in desperation is not attractive and does not instill confidence. I would also suggest that when you do decide to start looking to formally raise capital that you attack it as seriously as you would any internal project or program.

Aside from any early "friendly money" you raise from those closest in your network, it is statistically unlikely that any single meeting with any specific investor will eventually lead to a successful funding raise. You should anticipate that you will need to have dozens of meetings with different investors before you may receive any sign of interest, let alone a formal letter of interest (LOI) or term sheet.

Can you raise money by just pitching an idea (i.e., when pre-revenue)? It is certainly possible but not common unless you historically have had significant success and/or have access to an incredible network. If you're pitching an idea (aka "raising on the dream") you may be able to do it once—at the very beginning of your journey. Once you formally start, you'll need to provide more formal information (aka "raising on the data").

As you can't statistically rely on any single investor, it is best to try to maximize your chances by playing a numbers game. Ideally, you'll want to create a competitive environment among investors by running a formal process, using some version of these five steps:

First, prepare your pitch deck.

Second, identify which investors could have potential interest in your offering. Where possible, reach out through existing connections to the highest contacts you can at these firms. This may require that you do some significant historical research. What is their investment thesis? In what verticals do they typically invest? When was their most recent fund opened, and how far are they into their current fund? What were their last two or three investments and when were they made? Have they invested in your competitors? Do they lead investments or merely follow on after others?

This is as good a time as any to discuss venture syndication. Depending on the amount of funding that you're looking to raise, you might need to investigate a syndication deal, where there is more than one investor participating. I want to make a pointed distinction between lead investors and supporting/follower investors. Lead investors (almost obviously) usually perform most of the due diligence, typically set the terms for the deal, write the biggest check, and usually get a seat on the board of directors. Why would a VC that's leading an investment extend the deal to another firm? There are a few reasons. For one, they might be derisking the deal and diversifying to spread the risk. Second, they likely have an existing relationship with the other firm through some history. One other possibility is that an existing limited partner (LP) in their fund wishes to invest directly in addition to through the fund itself. The supporting/follower investors merely follow along with the lead investor; they cut a check and rely on the lead investor to oversee the company through their board seat.

You may find that once a lead investor has decided to fund your company, there will be no lack of interested secondary/follow-on investors, depending on the profile and historical return of the lead investor. There is generally no need to search for follower investors; the lead investor—if they wish to syndicate the deal—will source them for you. If they really like the terms of the deal, they will be loath to share with anyone else as bringing another firm into the structure of a syndicate could conceivably cause friction in the future.

My advice: look for investors who are willing to act as the lead investor on your deal.

As well, you will likely find a difference between investors whose careers started purely in finance versus those who used to be operators and then decided to start a VC. You might find that investors who once operated their own startup and successfully sold it before their career arc led them to VC will have more empathy and understanding of the challenges that founders have. Some may also refer to this as "smart money" for this very reason.

Third, prepare your more detailed materials (incorporation papers, cap table, org chart, team bios, sample contracts, investment memo, financial models, roadmap). Pending investor interest, these will need to be made available in what is called a "data room." I have seen one specific blog entry that states that you should never put together a data room; this view suggests that truly interested investors will fight tooth and nail to invest in your startup without one. I have not found this to be the case, however, and during the difficult times of unruly global macroeconomics, that is likely to be decidedly untrue.

Fourth, validate that you're ready, through warm introductions and ever-more-formal meetings, to increase and gauge interest in your startup. There is a certain amount of warm schmoozing that needs to go on during this process.

Fifth, formally complete the last round of the process ideally with multiple interested parties (in order to create a competitive market). Interested investors will have had a chance to review their options and possibly put together a letter of intent (LOI) stating the terms on which they would be interested in participating in investment.

These five steps can take three months or longer, and there is no guarantee that you will be successful in closing a deal by the end. Deals can be derailed at any point of the process.

Beware of so-called toxic term sheets. These usually include some blend of preferred stock, a senior liquidation preference, cumulative dividends, anti-dilution protection (in case of a down round), or guaranteed returns. These are more likely to be seen in later rounds rather than early rounds, but some unscrupulous investors try to slip them in pre-seed or seed rounds as well. I have seen one startup fail to receive a Series A round due to the fact that the previous round's lead investor had inserted anti-dilution protection that made any following investment wholly unattractive—the new investor's capital would grossly enrich the tranche of the last investor. Who wants to invest their own money to benefit someone else considerably more than themselves? If and when a term sheet is put forward, don't rely solely on your own judgment. Obtain excellent independent advice before signing *anything*.

You must recognize that if you are successful in finding an investor who wants to invest in your business at a priced round, it is likely that, in their mind, your company's valuation is considerably lower than what you have calculated in your head. It can be a serious blow to your ego. Consider the simple question: what is *anything* worth? In raw economic terms, any item is worth what someone is willing to pay for it. Prepare to be disappointed.

Why would an investor ultimately *not* be interested? There are a myriad of reasons with the biggest being: you simply did not catch their interest. They might have a conflict in their investment portfolio (such as a position in one of your competitors). They may not be comfortable investing in your vertical. They might believe that there's too much competition in your vertical (i.e., "it is crowded") and that you aren't sufficiently differentiated. They might not be comfortable with your corporate structure or the state of your cap table. They may perceive a personality conflict with someone on your management team. They may believe that the risk outweighs any possible benefit. Also, they might not be a "real" angel investor or investor at all but like to play-act at being one or present themselves to the outside world as an investor out of ego or to pretend they have cash on hand that they just do not. As a general rule, most serious angel investors don't need to slap "investor" or "angel investor" on their LinkedIn profiles.

As unfortunate as it can be, timing is likely to be the primary facet to gauge investor sentiment. Investors are very sensitive to the changing winds of momentum (including following the public market). A few years ago, cryptocurrency and Web3 plays were considered very interesting and received immense investments. In early 2023 with the emergence of ChatGPT, the school of fish quickly altered direction: more early-stage capital swam to invest in companies utilizing large language models (LLMs), and earlier hot ideas have cooled dramatically. By early 2025, I expect that much of the hype cycle of investing in LLMs and other generative AI will die down somewhat and be replaced with something else, such as superconductivity startups.

When you are doing your research investigating the investors you're looking to engage, I highly recommend that you also consider the primary performance metrics upon which venture capitalists and other investment firms are judged (specifically, by their own investors, sometimes known as limited partners or LPs) as this can be valuable to see if they're the right fit. In addition to any particular fund's stage or risk profile, the two key metrics are MOIC and IRR (definitions forthcoming).

Let's say that any particular fund will invest in ten companies. As I've said previously, an investment firm will have a specific lifetime in mind for each specific fund. Early in a fund's existence, it may have more latitude in both the size and type of investment they're able to support. You may need to do some legwork in piecing together what investments have been made from within any specific investor's fund. You will find that it is opaque at best, though there are some websites that have aggregated some of this information. I suggest that *Crunchbase* is a good place to start.

Coupled with their fund stage is their risk profile. If you can determine what other companies are currently held within this specific fund, you may be able to get a better sense of their risk profile and appetite to see if your company fits appropriately.

Regarding the key metrics I've mentioned:

MOIC stands for "multiple of invested capital." It is one metric used to calculate an investor's return on investment (specifically, the multiple achieved).

MOIC = (Realized value + Unrealized value)/Total dollar amount invested

For example, if $1 was invested and the total value was $5, the MOIC is 5x.

Note that time is *not* factored into this calculation.

IRR stands for internal rate of return. It represents the interest rate that sets the net present value of cash flows to zero. It is not simple to calculate manually; use Excel or any number of IRR calculators available online.

For example, if $1 was invested and the total value was $5, the IRR is 37.9 percent.

Unlike MOIC, time is factored into the calculation of IRR. In either case, higher numbers are preferred. While a high MOIC can certainly be impressive, if the same (high) multiple is achieved in less time, that is likely preferential.

You may not be able to discover any fund's MOIC or IRR—they're usually kept under wraps. Yet I trust that the most motivated among you will find a way to find them.

Here might be some surprising news for you: the overwhelming majority of startups never manage to raise external capital at all (I am including friends-and-family money in the category of "internal" capital). Those who do manage to raise their first external round do not necessarily survive long enough to raise a second external round. There are no guarantees, and the capital raise itself doesn't automatically confer success. You may need to keep wearing the Chief Survival Officer hat for quite some time. This isn't necessarily a bad thing—imagine you spend two decades gradually and organically growing a business to sell it at a life-changing valuation where you own the vast majority of the company—that doesn't seem to me like a poor outcome whatsoever. Especially when you compare what it looks like if you are successful in raising external capital.

To that point, if you do manage to successfully raise external capital, I have a warning. External capital is not patient capital. The funding that you receive from investors comes at a price; a clock starts ticking, and they would like to see a return on investment—they have their own investors from whom they raised this capital (or made commitments to fund within a specific timeline), and those investors, in turn, demand a return. If you do manage to raise capital, be judicious in spending it. There may be a tendency to go hog-wild once the taps have been sprung open. I recommend being as frugal during each round as you were in the beginning. Money is just a tool—intended to amplify and magnify your reach. Running a capital raise process is difficult, and it gets more difficult and involved with each successive round. The stakes are higher, the demands are higher, and the parties larger and more involved.

Once you jump on the capital raise bandwagon, there will need to be a decision made regarding the eventual state of the company. The company may wish to remain private or perhaps sell to a strategic buyer or enter the public market by IPO. During the dot-com era, the IPO was broadly seen as the default vehicle for corporate success, and dozens of companies foolishly went public by that route and eventually flamed out.

In a repeat of the dot-bomb flameout, companies that went public via a special purpose acquisition company (SPAC) vehicle ultimately provided a similar variation on the flameout theme in the early 2020s, with a similar impact befalling the retail investor attracted to these firms.

I have no first-hand experience bringing a company to the public market, but it seems that it is a compliance hornet's nest. If you thought that you were under scrutiny from your investors previously, in the words of Al Jolson: "You ain't seen nothin' yet." There are significant benefits to keeping your company private longer. There are many examples of companies that go public but then in later years return to the private market (usually through strategic acquisition or to PE companies). In any case, an IPO shouldn't be considered a destination in itself. It is merely a milestone and shouldn't be your ultimate goal any more than building a business with a "unicorn" valuation should be. *If* you do happen to build a business and it achieves "unicorn" status and/or you take it public, do not expect this to happen within a few years of your start.

My final quip in this section is something I heard at a cocktail event for founders: "Congratulating someone on their capital raise is like congratulating the chef on buying the groceries." It is important, but ultimately, executional excellence trumps all.

Chasing an investment to grow your business is serious business, and it requires significant time and effort on your part. If you must raise capital, try to do so on your own terms and from a position of strength—if you wait until you desperately need external capital, it is increasingly likely that you will not successfully raise it. Also, do not expect that a successful capital raise will solve all problems. Sales is a vastly greater cure-all for any company's pain than is outside investment capital.

# CHAPTER 22

# Post-Financing, or How Money Magnifies Issues

I HAVE READ THE WISE words of a gentleman named Steve Cheney, the Cofounder of Estimote. Cheney coined a very interesting rule regarding raising capital: "For every dollar you receive from an investor, you should plan on returning ten dollars. On the other hand, every dollar you receive from a client (through sales) is worth five dollars from an investor." The best money you can ever raise is through sales—period.

As well, I have coined my own rule about money: "Money can only solve the problems that money can solve." Problems encountered in life (including startup life) are rarely solved wholly by an influx of money. If your team is dysfunctional, money will not help it in the long term. Indeed, it may further magnify existing problems that had been previously unearthed. When you see lesser competitors that have raised significant amounts of capital in comparison to you, put that in perspective and focus on what is real: money can buy you time, but it can't buy you operational excellence.

Two specific examples of the problems that often arise after a successful capital raise may include those of demands and jealousy. First, demands. People within the company might feel that they have a right to that sudden influx of capital. During your capital raise you needed to provide in detail the "use of proceeds"; don't deviate from your plans. You will find that strangers will swarm your LinkedIn profile with connection requests. Second, jealousy. Those who have never walked the startup founder path may see a successful corporate fundraise as money that went directly into your pocket. That isn't the case (unless you've taken a secondary financing) but that doesn't necessarily change perception. This may be true for both employees and those external to your company. It will need to be managed, and it's your job as Chief Survival Officer to communicate this proactively and clearly to your team.

If you are successful in raising outside capital and your company proceeds down the path with successive rounds of financing, recognize that you will undoubtedly experience friction between existing investors and new investors. At best you may find there may be an uneasy alliance between investors, even if they are in the same tranche. Expect a level of "co-opetition" as they will each want to see you succeed but to the primary and direct benefit of *themselves*. Anticipate that successive rounds of investment will demand preferential treatment (possibly including but not exclusive to liquidation preferences) that may raise the ire of earlier investors. At this stage, it can feel like you are watching your investors play *Star Trek*-style three-dimensional chess, and you're Spock, equipped with special sensors to detect the emotions that trigger their moves on the chessboard.

On the other hand, you may close an investment round, but ultimately you may be unsuccessful regarding execution upon the promised use of the associated proceeds. For example, your investment thesis may have committed you to invest the proceeds in partnership sales personnel and in engineering talent dedicated to partnership integrations. However, due to labor market conditions or business exigencies, you failed to hire the people you said you would. Building out partnerships to scale revenues may have been central to the reason people invested in you. When this failure to execute on your promise reveals itself, existing investors may be loath to invest more capital—period. It may even be necessary for you to raise a "down round": the equivalent of dollar-cost averaging (DCA) in the private market. Every successive equity round dilutes the previous equity rounds, and, given the preferential terms of the new deal, it may seem punitive—especially to the common shareholders (generally, the founders and employees). Issuing further options grants for these earlier shareholders may soften the sting of this kind of dilution, but a down round will undoubtedly demoralize and disincentivize your fellow employees.

You'll find that there's a definite need to regularly keep in touch with your investors. Seasoned investors will very often require a seat on a formal board of directors, and you should expect to have regular quarterly meetings with them, and you'll need to allocate significant time spent preparing for these meetings, including one-on-one calls. No "bad news" should come as a surprise at the formal business meeting since bad news for board member investors, and for all board members, gets worse the longer it is withheld. If you've raised an earlier round with angels, I still recommend that you maintain regular contact with them to keep them apprised of your business trajectory. A quarterly cadence set early and maintained will be good for your muscle memory. Being prepared for board meetings will make your investors feel confident in your growth. They want to share in your success; they'd like to know early if there are problems so that they can assist. Nobody likes having a surprise dropped on them, especially if you need them to help bail you out when your boat runs aground and starts to leak.

## ANGEL INVESTMENT STALLED

*One of my earliest small angel investments in someone else's startup started before the "global reset" of 2020; the company in question was significantly impacted. Unfortunately, they went radio silent for many quarters until late 2022, when suddenly a flurry of emails and webcast updates were sent out. I joined the webcast; they announced their new "slimmed down" company and new product updates, and at the end, it was clear they had "buried the lede": they were asking for another capital raise. Their bank had called their business line of credit, and they had a very short time to cover it.*

*Despite being eerily common, this is a terrible way to communicate with your investors. The webcast itself felt like a pitch to new investors; they didn't acknowledge existing investors, and as such it felt a bit disrespectful.*

*Angels, more so than other classes of investors, are generally investing their own capital, upon which they've already paid taxes. They're taking a huge personal and reputational risk in investing in your dream, and if you don't treat them with the respect they deserve, you can be guaranteed that they will not support you going forward. And downstream institutional investors may ask: "What happened to your fanatical angel investors? Have they lost faith in you? Why?"*

Money, we see, does not solve all startup problems; you should expect that if you're successful in a capital raise, entirely new problems will crop up as a result. You're now held accountable to another group (in addition to your employees), and this group will express a clear timeline and return-on-investment expectations.

# CHAPTER 23

# Moving from a Startup to a Scale-Up Mindset

LET'S PROJECT INTO THE FUTURE: you have executed well on your plans, pivoted when necessary, and have acquired a strong following of employees and clients along the way. Congratulations! You're likely at the cusp of transitioning from a startup to a scale-up.

To quote legendary executive leadership coach and author Marshall Goldsmith: "What got you here won't get you there." You likely won't be able to rely on your previously acquired muscle memory and actions to move into scale-up mode.

What are the biggest stumbling blocks when moving from a small startup mode to a considerably larger scale-up mode? There are many, including the following:

Leadership and Team Dynamics. I have written much about the leadership team, with the focus on the founder(s) and the dynamics therein. You will find that as a founder, you'll need to shift the team dynamics: you will undoubtedly struggle with delegating tasks and then ensuring that the entire team is aligned to the company's shifting goals and vision—especially as the team expands. Preserving and even enhancing your firm's current culture will likely be the most difficult challenge. Culture undoubtedly contributed significantly to your success thus far. As the team grows, you will find it even more difficult to keep everyone informed and connected; you will encounter communication challenges you never found before.

Scaling of Operations. The necessity of scaling operations lays bare existing technical debt, which can be significant. This will likely include both infrastructure rigidity/creakiness and associated warts in process optimization. You will need to ensure that your technical infrastructure can handle an increased customer data load. Similarly, the strength of your original innovation team will need to be nurtured along with the growth (so you don't become moribund). I appreciate the phrase: "Nail it before you scale it."

Financial Management. As I have alluded to before, "cash flow is king," and maintaining a healthy cash flow becomes even more important than ever before. You will need to expand your finance team to plan for the scaling endeavor. As well, if you've been able to raise money in the early stages, you will find that the formal process of raising the next rounds will be considerably more onerous.

Customer Acquisition and Retention. As you move from a small startup to a larger entity, you will discover that current customers may be displeased. Yes, they want you to succeed but will likely miss some of the early days when you as the founder were able to commit more focused and personal time with them. In fact, the very market test of whether you are in scale-up mode is whether you, as founder, are not stickhandling the many jobs you held during your startup phase: customer success lead, head of sales, head of partnerships, HR lead, head of PR, and head of innovation. You cannot personally scale yourself; you will need to find methodologies to retain these customers as well as acquiring new ones. Similarly, your marketing and sales processes will need to scale to reach broader markets without compromising existing efficacy.

Market Dynamics and Global Expansion. You will undoubtedly need to pivot out from your original market and move to adjacent markets. This may also demand expansion outside of your original geographic regions. You will find that existing strategies will need to be updated to meet the clients in these different markets and geographies. You will undoubtedly discover that these different business environments come along with challenges in regulatory rules, culture, and different sets of business risks.

Amid this evolution, you will need to be open-minded, resilient, and thoughtful when embracing the change to move the company from startup to scale-up mode. As a founder, you will need to recognize and avoid the well-known "founder's dilemma."[2]

---

2  Coined by Noam Wasserman, one such dilemma is striking a careful balance between maintaining control and attracting the best resources to grow the startup, as the easy short-term choice might well be the most perilous in the long run. See Wasserman, N. (2013). *The Founder's Dilemmas: Anticipating and Avoiding the Pitfalls That Can Sink a Startup*. Princeton University Press.

# CHAPTER 24

# When Things Fall Apart (with Gratitude to Pema Chödron)

*"You must go on. I can't go on. I'll go on."*

—Samuel Beckett, *The Unnamable*

C LINICAL WARNING: I WANT to remind you that I am neither a trained counselor nor a mental health professional. My advice and coping mechanisms may not work for you. Mental fortitude is a difficult thing to harness. It is quite possible that when you find yourself in the midst of a mental health issue that none of these words will have any impact or value to you. If you are suicidal, please seek trained medical assistance immediately.

"Hustle culture" as described in the media and on X (formerly, Twitter) usually focuses on the shiny exterior view of success (Lambos! Boats! Fancy suits! Beachfront properties! Hotels in the south of France! Fat stacks of cash!) of survivor bias and rarely exposes the dark underbelly of an entrepreneurial life, especially the early startup days.

You should expect that despite whatever success you achieve at some point, things will fall apart. Most of what I have put together in this book I learned along the path through the various mishaps, bumps, and bruises that come along with nurturing a startup. Unless you're incredibly lucky, you're going to discover exactly how much resilience you have—almost to the breaking point—and perhaps you'll cross into that territory.

You may discover that you can't make the next payroll.

You may discover that a key employee has submitted their resignation papers, and they will be departing in two weeks' time, leaving you high and dry, with committed work or deadlines that can't be achieved.

You might get the call that a beloved fellow employee has been in an accident and is not expected to survive.

I have experienced each of these.

You may even find that a superset of these (and more!) occur simultaneously.

As well, you might discover some personal issues that impair your hustle has sucker-punched you in your life. Startup life doesn't shield you from your personal life. In fact, these lives will bleed into each other. As an example, perhaps your focus on the startup has precipitated a crack in the personal relationship with your spouse, partner, or sibling.

How do you move forward?

Again, think back to the Chief Survival Officer mode. Much of startup life is simply surviving yet another day until you catch a lucky break.

In this context, the old term "incubators" (now supplanted by "accelerators") for startups is appropriate. Most startups could not survive without external support and care. But even with the assistance of others, you cannot wholly rely upon external factors to save you.

You will need to dig deep.

You will need to find something to bring you back to the surface when it feels like you're drowning when you are at your most vulnerable.

## STRESS IS 13/10

*After a particularly difficult and long day at work, I returned home. Lying on my bed and staring up at the ceiling, I thought I was having a heart attack. My wife called telehealth; I spoke to a nurse who strongly recommended that I go to the hospital immediately. I was rapidly triaged through the emergency room, and the hospital staff performed some tests (it was astounding to see how quickly medical personnel responded when a male in his mid-30s arrived at the ER complaining of chest pain). While waiting for the results, I sat alone in the hospital room quietly crying, thinking about my family and how I was going to leave my daughter without a father. The results soon came back: no indications of enzymes characteristic of a heart attack. Luckily, it was merely a panic attack. I remember the doctor giving me the results and asking me, "On a scale of 1 to 10, what is the stress level in your life?" My reply: "13."*

*This was an eye-opener, and obviously this could not continue. The startup had been my sole focus for so long that I needed some external outlet for stress release, and I absolutely needed to make time for it—STAT. This was my first entrance into the study of Aikido. Aikido has helped me in innumerable ways. It has given me the tools to help me better cope with stress by enhancing my overall physical fitness; it touches on facets of anger management and on dealing with interpersonal confrontation and interaction. My study of Aikido over the years has worked wonders for me across all these dimensions of life.*

Immense stress is practically inevitable in the startup journey so I believe it is critical that you find some coping mechanism that works to balance your life as best you can. Whichever coping mechanism you choose, it is essential that you schedule and prioritize regular sessions to disconnect and regain your balance. I would strongly suggest that recreational drugs (including alcohol) not be your go-to coping mechanism. I believe they are an unsustainable crutch and ultimately will hinder your survival. I enjoy a tipple myself from time to time (especially when in a social environment), but it can be a slippery slope, particularly if you have a genetic tendency toward addiction.

Avoid self-medicating with depressants (especially alcohol) as a tonic for your stress.

Try different things to see what works for you. Spend scheduled time with your family. Reach out to other founders for moral support. Join a group that supports charitable efforts—be useful to others. Go to a place of worship if you believe spiritual guidance will help. Exercise! Crank motivational music until the speakers sizzle. Listen to motivational speeches from Simon Sinek or Mel Robbins. Speak with your friends who are outside the startup ecosystem—they can help provide perspective and balance. Try some of Dutch motivational speaker and extreme athlete Wim "The Iceman" Hoff's breathing exercises to settle your nerves. To ground you further, some works by the Stoics, like Seneca or Epictetus, who help orient you in terms of how you fit as a bit player, but an important player, in a larger universe unfolding. The title of this chapter was lifted in whole from the book of the same name by Pema Chödron, a prolific American Tibetan-Buddhist instructor whose insights into Buddhism I have appreciated for years.

A good psychotherapist can help in many respects across both your personal and work lives (and let's face it—in a startup, they're pretty much inextricably intertwined). One key use of therapy is to help the patient gain a better understanding of themselves, their motivators, and blind spots to heal past traumas. Cognitive behavioral therapy (CBT) is one specific form of therapy that is highly structured, problem focused, and goal oriented. Unsurprisingly, this can be a very attractive option for startup founders dealing with depression or other anxiety disorders. More recently tools derived from a school of psychology known as dialectical behavior therapy (DBT) developed in the 1990s by Dr. Marsha Linehan. DBT is based on the principles of CBT but extends its focus on emotional and social aspects; an evidence-based approach intended to help people improve their distress tolerance, and to regulate and cope with their emotions, In his book *Outlive*, Dr. Peter Attia notes that DBT is not a passive modality, that it requires conscious thought and action on a daily basis.

He also recommends the use of simple interventions that stimulate the vagus nerve to induce a parasympathetic mode to help refocus (such as a cold shower or stepping into an ice bath). I have also found that acupuncture gives astounding results. At the end of a good acupuncture session, I feel like I've been completely reset from a cold reboot.

With the words of the Stoics in mind, eventually you will recognize that you need to let go of what you cannot possibly change or control. While my suggestions in the previous paragraphs might sound hokey, let me give you some examples. If I am in a depressive mental state, I can make choices to move forward (even slightly) instead of just maintaining the current path. Get out of bed as soon as you wake up. Listen to some music that is inspirational instead of depressing. Look: I think that Radiohead's "*OK Computer*" is one of the best albums ever made—but it is *not* what I should be listening to if I'm feeling depressed or exhausted. Any activity or influence that moves the needle a bit toward the positive ledger of mental health is a bonus for me.

---

### ELDON'S STARTUP HYPE LIST

*Lose Yourself*—Eminem

*Woke Up This Morning*—Alabama 3

*99 Problems*—JAY-Z

*Get Up Offa That Thing*—James Brown

*Money*—The Flying Lizards

*Don't Call Us, We'll Call You*—Sugarloaf

*C.R.E.A.M.*—Wu Tang Clan

*Started from the Bottom*—Drake

---

When it comes to a positive mental health mindset, consistency is more important than infrequent and sketchy efforts. Even mindful eating of essentially good food can help you achieve and maintain a semblance of balance (minimizing sugar and over-processed carbohydrate intake can help avoid insulin crashes). If you can find a support group of others in the same situation, you may find that could help.

If possible, do try to shield the vast majority of your stress and pressure from your fellow employees. It is unfair for you to unburden yourself of every minor issue that arises on them. If you choose to do so, you shouldn't be surprised if they abandon your enterprise in fear (to find an ostensibly safer haven in another company). The stresses of a startup are such that the average person cannot truly empathize unless they have walked the path themselves. Even employees quite dedicated to the company, when exposed to the raw uncertainty and stress from a startup, will feel a concerted urge to protect themselves and their families. None of this should be surprising to you. I'm not saying that you must hide the truth from them. I appreciate what the late Daniel Kahneman said about the cognitive biases of entrepreneurs: "The blessings of optimism are offered only to individuals who . . . are able to 'accentuate the positive' without losing track of reality."

In this same vein, if you find yourself in financial difficulty, do not hide this from your investors. They are your partners in this endeavor; if you need assistance, be forthright and give them plenty of time to see if they can arrange some alternative form of financing to bring you through these difficult times. As a specific ideal example, this could be some form of non-dilutive financing such as a bridge loan. Financial restructuring can take considerable time to effect; if you send out a call for help too late, there may not be a way to rescue you.

Aside from the ethical difficulties of running a company when you're low on cash, there are serious legal issues to take into consideration. In many jurisdictions, failing to pay employees when the employer is aware of the inability to do so can lead to legal consequences, including potential charges of fraud. In addition to your investors, other stakeholders need to be looped in to work out options (including reducing wages, offering additional equity in lieu of current salary, or permitting fellow employees to start looking for other jobs). As terrible as this option is, you might find that this refocuses the team as they all begin to fight hard for the company's survival.

Aside from the human stresses of running a business, you will likely find, with time, that the customer acquisition strategies that worked so well in the past aren't working anymore. It may be tempting to wholly abandon your current strategy to try something completely different. Unless you haven't had any success whatsoever, I would suggest that you *pivot* instead of *hop* to another strategy. Build on the experience that you've accumulated to date. Is there an approach that's adjacent to your current strategy? Look at what you've built so far and see what has led to sustained positive traction. What made this specific strategic route achieve better results than others? A subtle change in strategy and/or tactics might help to clear that logjam.

Perhaps you've fallen into a bit of a rut—you've lost interest in this project for any number of reasons. One possibility is that when you move through your founder-to-scale-up journey, you're required to take on more managerial responsibility rather than the more technical aspects you thrived on at the very beginning. You fell in love with a technology solution; that propelled you to start and grow the business and you're now being asked to leave that role behind. Do you miss exercising your "technical acumen" muscle because you've been spending increasing amounts of time developing your business acumen? Perhaps it is time to start looking for professional managerial assistance so you can refocus on the technical aspects you love (and that you've missed because you've been running the show, wearing so many hats for so long).

Throughout the most difficult years of eSentire (and I'm referring specifically to the first several), I would always say, "If this *thing* of ours doesn't work out, it won't be because we didn't try hard enough." My cofounder and I had fully committed to it—we were single-minded and dedicated to its success, especially through the earliest and most challenging times. But as I've said throughout, effort does not necessarily guarantee success.

Now, let's say that you are near the breaking point in one or more points of your life. Is it time to call it quits? I don't know—only you can tell. Again, numerous studies show that the vast majority of startups fail in fewer than ten years. Specifically, it appears that half of all startups fail between years four and six of their inception. For some people, failure is a badge of honor, especially in the high-churn environments of the Bay Area. There are significant opportunity costs as a founder when you're trying to run a business you've started. The entire endeavor can be exhausting, and the option to leave it all behind may very well be enticing. I would guess that it might be easier to wind down your startup if you're younger (e.g., under 35 years) rather than older as you might see other more interesting opportunities suddenly available to you.

Another possibility: let's say that you've put five years of effort into your startup and you're doing well but not quite at the point that you wanted to be. Again, I would suggest that you carefully ponder the outcomes you most desire. Recognize that as we get older, our priorities change. Consider where you are now rather than where you started—this may help you decide whether you want to persevere or fold it. It might be time to look at selling the business outright and stay on as an advisor for two years to aid in the transition. "Rational perseverance" is the phrase that comes to mind.

I'm not sure there's any easy answer to this. Sometimes in your position as the Chief Survival Officer, you need to make the painful decision to depart and survive to fight a different battle another day.

There are startups that I have seen led by fantastic founders, a solid team, and an interesting core of an idea but that were not able to make it work for other reasons—being too far ahead of the market, facing global macroeconomic headwinds, and other market timing issues. Their current venture may not have succeeded, but the next venture will likely have a better chance at survival—if they learned the lessons on offer.

If you finally do choose to wind down your startup, you will be surprised at the outpouring of support you will find. You will likely dread the conversations you need to make—especially to investors. If your investors were originally operators (i.e., founders) themselves, you might be overwhelmed by the amount of empathy and sympathy you receive. Do not be surprised if they commiserate and suggest that you take some time to regroup. After you have had a chance to dust yourself off, they will likely ask you what you're going to do next. Good people want to work with other good people repeatedly—let's call it "getting the band back together." The accumulated knowledge you have learned along the way will be put to good use—and hopefully, you recognize looming problems ahead of time and better understand how to trim the sails.

*A few years ago, I attended a sweat lodge hosted by an indigenous family in northern Ontario. Throughout the ceremony they gave thanks to those who came before us—our ancestors. The experience resonated with me. My maternal grandfather, Zinko Daviskiba, was a tenant farmer in Zelenij Rog, a small village south of Kiev and east of Uman (in Ukraine), and had immigrated to Canada in the early 1900s to claim land in Hallebourg (near Hearst) in northern Ontario. I cannot fathom what that struggle was like: abandoning family, traveling in a decidedly unglamorous style, without prior knowledge of the English language, heading to a wild and frozen territory to start anew. I am grateful to my ancestors for their struggle to improve their lives, and my own trials pale in comparison. When you are at a low point, find your own personal inspiration wherever you can to fight on.*

*Whatever our circumstances are, we are the living embodiment of our ancestors' dreams.*

Given enough time, you *will* encounter problems. Many may be well outside of your own sphere of control. Develop survival skills to cope with them—the earlier, the better. Rational perseverance coupled with an honest self-assessment might help to make difficult yet necessary decisions regarding you and your startup's future.

# CHAPTER 25

# Surviving Success

S
UCCESS IS ELUSIVE. Success is wriggly. Success is slippery.

If you find yourself grinding, setting goals, and reaching them (despite setbacks), you will find that your definition of success keeps moving the goalposts beyond your grasp.

Let's use a simple example: in sales, the first million dollars of revenue your company reaches is the hardest to achieve. But once you reach that goal, you'll find that the second million is easier. To that end, let's briefly discuss the BHAG again. The whole idea behind establishing a BHAG is to set a goal that you yourself would have difficulty believing that it is achievable. That's exactly the point. You're supposed to have it as your North Star; your reach should exceed your grasp.

Of course, you'll need to set smaller goals to build upon that will help you reach your BHAG. Ideally, you'll want to establish a flywheel sales and customer delivery process that automatically feeds and self-perpetuates your growth—some single, atomic item that can be readily duplicated at scale with a positive return on investment. The flywheel, in other words, is what helps "make you money when you sleep."

The secret is: *you* get to define your own measure of success. It may very well be a sales figure. It may very well be happy employees helping to build an excellent product. It may be material comfort in a family business. It may be setting up your children for generational wealth. Perhaps, for some, it *is* the Instagram manifestation of hustle culture success: first-class airplane pods (or better yet, your own jet!), flashy fancy cars (Lambos! Ferraris!), three-star Michelin restaurant meals, exotic vacations in the south of France, a lavish estate in Grand Cayman, huge diamond-encrusted timepieces, and fat stacks of cash. If that's your style, there's nothing wrong with it. I'm saying that *you* (and you alone) get to define it, and you get to change it along the way as appropriate. Move the goalposts as you need.

You will find that you will need to be consistent in your effort. As an entrepreneur committed, you need to continually exercise The Will to execute repeatedly.

You will need to be continually creative in your thinking and execution, repeatedly so.

You may find that you started the business so that you're no longer under the thumb of "The Man" only to discover to your surprise that your clients each vie aggressively for your time and that, in your employees' eyes, *you* are "The Man." Never mind that. Transcend it.

Somewhere along the line, as you find and savor each manifestation of success, you can change your title from being the Chief Survival Officer to the Chief Success Officer.

If you do reach a certain level of success, you will undoubtedly find that there will be people arriving at the company to whom you need to hand over the keys. Note that your investors will undoubtedly drive this process. Remember that while they believe in you and your offering, they're more concerned with growth. It may be "growth at all costs" versus "sustainable growth" but remember the metrics that are most important to their limited partners—and those metrics demand growth results.

Not everyone gets to be Mark Zuckerberg, who started and remains the CEO, chairman, and controlling shareholder of the company they started. You may find a twinge of ego and hurt in this realization. You're not alone. Jack Dorsey, founding CEO of Twitter (now X), said that being asked to step down was akin to being punched in the stomach.

Professor Noam Wasserman, when at Harvard (he is now the dean of business at Yeshiva University), described this dilemma as he posed the question, "Do you want to be rich, or do you want to be king?" If you choose the former, you most likely need to give up control of "your baby" (that nobody will love as much as you do). If you choose the latter, you manage to keep control, but you take the chance of your business never succeeding in the way that it could under more professional management. As well, under your reign, the business may even die in the process.

Wasserman found that about 80 percent of founder-CEOs actively resisted giving up control. This is wholly unsurprising to me; having devoted so much time and energy into the endeavor, having taken outsized risks and passing up other opportunities, the company becomes an essential part of your body. I sometimes joke in saying that I had so frequently introduced myself as "Eldon Sprickerhoff, eSentire" that the company name had subsumed my surname.

As a founder, if you're successful, you'll need to prepare to face this eventuality. The company outgrowing your own competency is like your child outgrowing your need for helicopter parenting: it is more than a little sad, but it can be a very beautiful thing if you prepare for this eventuality. And, most importantly, don't let your ego get in the way. Many startups don't survive the move to scale-up mode.

Expect that once you achieve a certain level of material success, you will have people knocking on your door requesting money—either for philanthropic efforts or for you to fund their startup dream. Use the specific knowledge that you have acquired throughout your own struggles and be especially judicious with your use of proceeds.

So you may need to calibrate and regularly re-calibrate your definition of success. There comes a point where expensive and showy physical goods lose their luster.

# CHAPTER 26

# *Memento Mori* So C2MF

*"Art is long, life is short, and success is very far off."*

—Joseph Conrad

W E MAY DISAGREE ON any number of specific details, but one thing is for certain: we are not here for very long. The Latin phrase *Memento Mori* roughly translates to "Remember that you will die." I am a huge fan of the Irish author Samuel Beckett. One of the key themes in his writing is the passage of time—none of us can escape it.

So, to that end, if you truly believe in this endeavor of yours, you must commit fully to it, punch the accelerator, and take it as far as it can go. Make carefully considered choices to maximize gains while minimizing risk but execute while you still can.

There is one final point I'd like to make: there is a huge difference between reading Shakespeare's magnificent play, *Hamlet*, versus performing the lead role on stage in front of a thousand people. As Hamlet himself says in Act 2, Scene 2: "The Play's the Thing." Does Hamlet mean that only acting, being, in the live performance can reveal life's hidden truths and realities? I think so. It is one thing to read this book and an entirely different thing to execute in a committed fashion.

I have suggested reading material throughout this book (and at the end, too); there are many excellent lessons and road rules for startups, but ultimately none of it matters unless you put the advice to the test.

For inspiration, I am reminded of the Schott family slogan, "You Can't Do Business Sitting on Your Ass" (YCDBSOYA). I myself prefer my personal credo of "Chop Chop, My Friend" (C2MF). Reading this and the other materials I've suggested can help, but ultimately, you'll need to do the hard work to be committed.

To that end, I hope that I've been able to give you some inspiration, identify pitfalls, and encourage you to move forward in a more focused manner along your startup journey.

If you disagree with something that I've said, I hope that you prove me wrong. Nothing would make me happier than to discover that you didn't take my advice—nay, actually did the exact opposite of what I suggested—but it worked out well for you in spite of it!

Chop Chop, My Friends. Each of us doesn't have a lot of time left. Be committed to win.

*"Take what you need, and be on your way."*
—OASIS

# ACKNOWLEDGMENTS

# With Gratitude

T HE IDEAS AND CORE talking points supporting this book sprung from a presentation that I first gave when accepting the J. W. Graham Medal in "Computing and Innovation" from the University of Waterloo in 2019. As part of the events spread across two days, I was asked to speak at the university's Recognizing Excellence Summit, along with several others (including two Turing Award Laureates), and felt woefully out of place. Though I had cofounded a very successful information security services company and had come up with some novel products and offerings, from an academic perspective, I had made no significant advances in mathematics. Truth be told, I was a somewhat mediocre and diffident student during my time at the University of Waterloo. One specific incident stands out: in my 1B term, I took a class in assembly language, in which the teaching assistants told me that I was the worst programmer they'd ever encountered (although to be fair, the code undeniably worked so that counts for something!).

Nevertheless, I had promised to speak for about half an hour; I figured that I could discuss my "blind spots" from starting a tech company in a serious global recession through almost two decades (from startup to scale-up). The ambitious title I chose was "The Accidental Entrepreneurd: A Pocket MBA in 30 Minutes or Less," and I first had to correct the spellcheck as it repeatedly "fixed" the deliberately misspelled title. I did not in fact offer any pocket MBA at the conclusion of the talk, but the points from that original thirty-minute talk have expanded into this more in-depth effort with, I hope, considerably more heft and value.

I need to thank my unindicted co-conspirators: my long-suffering wife Carole and our daughter Siobhan, for their support throughout this entrepreneurial journey. Whatever success I have had as an entrepreneurd is due in great part to them. I would like to thank my parents for fostering my lifelong love of reading, emphasizing the need for an education, and demonstrating the value of consistent effort.

I am most grateful to Andrew Rosson, my first "True Believer" client, who repeatedly gave me access to sandboxes in which I could play and test my earliest ideas. Along with being our "Johnny Appleseed" spreading the word of eSentire's offerings during the earliest days of the company, I have counted on Andrew to be a tremendous mentor and friend throughout my journey.

In a similar vein, I am also most grateful to J. Paul Haynes, the first CEO of eSentire, as a particularly committed and invested mentor who brought his significant business acumen to a floundering enterprise and radically changed its trajectory for the better through his efforts.

I am grateful to the so-called Elders of Eldon, the first dozen friends who encouraged and supported me early on in my journey: Kristoffer Stack, Arthur Vaccarino (who tragically passed away during the editing phase of this book), Mark Van Der Sande, Kevin Moran, Charles Kim, Christopher Moskowitz, Kurt Brungardt, Mark Kuron, Jon Rotter, Len Lombardo, and Chris Turek.

I am grateful to the entire team at eSentire for executing in such a professional and effective manner to allow me to take a summer sabbatical and begin formulating the writing process without intense external pressures. A company's impact can be derived from the vector sum of its employees: both past and present. I would like to specifically thank Kerry Bailey and Chris Gesell for taking the reins back in 2018 and lead the charge to help move eSentire far into the scale-up zone of commercial success. Without the company being in their most capable hands, I could not have felt comfortable in formally stepping back from the day-to-day operations and adjusting to take on new challenges. Their individual skill sets far eclipse mine, and when I hear people talk about the astounding company of eSentire, I just say, "I was there at the beginning, and despite the obvious and almost insurmountable obstacles I was too unrealistically determined, pig-headed and foolish to realize that it couldn't work. I persevered and kept going until truly capable people came in and helped me to propel it forward." I mean that. I am happy to have been able to come along for the ride, and along the way absorb so much of their knowledge and insight to be able to detail my perspectives in this tome.

I am grateful for those who took the time and read (and even re-read) early versions of this writing project, including Valerie Wagg, Sumit Bhatia, Kristi Kanitz, Leigh Honeywell, Brian Bourne, Ethan Smart, James Mignacca, Jeff Sims, Nick Aleks, Mario Vodopivec, Nick Scozzaro, Penelope Stevens, Benjamin Saberin, Nadia Mazzarolo, Erin McLean, and Alex Tong for their invaluable criticisms, suggestions, and corrections.

I would especially like to thank Jane Podbelskaya for her focused and practical advice regarding specific details within the early-stage fundraising process. Many thanks to Sydney Druckman for her patience with my many changes, edits, and additions.

Finally, I would like to thank Rick Howard, Mahendra Ramsinghani, Bob Seeman, and Neil Seeman for their inspiring advice and immense patience regarding my many novice questions regarding the aspects and mechanics of the publishing world.

Any errors discovered within this text are wholly mine.

# TL;DR

You'd better love what you do—as much as
you'd love one of your own children.

———

If you build a better mousetrap, the world will not
simply beat a path to your front door.

———

Everything will take longer than you expect it to,
even when you take this statement into account.

———

All of the easy work has already been done,
some of it even by you.

———

Become aware of your blind spots.

———

You can't expect everyone will love your baby
(the company) as much as you do.

———

Hard work isn't likely going to be enough.

———

Learn how to sell. Do not abdicate the responsibility for selling.

———

You will need money to survive. Cash flow is king.

———

You will need to dig deep inside and find The Will to push on.

———

Become uncomfortably comfortable with vulnerability.

———

We live in a VUCA world: volatile, uncertain,
complex, ambiguous.

---

You'll need to get used to getting your heart broken, repeatedly.

---

Your first salesperson is incredibly critical to
your success (or failure).

---

When hiring, find people who are AAA: available,
amicable, and able—in that order.

---

Hire slowly, fire quickly.

---

When delegating, recognize that the hardest part
of love is letting go, but neither you nor your
fellow employees will grow if you don't.

---

Find your "true believer" customers and consider
their perspective on an ongoing basis. Bend over
backward to make them succeed.

---

Spell out the "characteristics of our best clients."

---

Founder authenticity is a superpower.

---

Regarding startup accelerators, be coachable, do the work,
eschew groupthink, make connections.

---

Beware of unmarried marriage counselors.

---

You cannot wait for investors to find you
and your pre-revenue company.

---

Significant growth will eventually require capital.

---

Seasoned investors will evaluate your company on five characteristics: the team, the offering, the numbers, your customers, and the broader market.

---

Steve Cheney's rule of money: Money from sales is at least 10x more valuable than money from investors.

---

Eldon Sprickerhoff's rule of money: Money can only solve the problems money can solve.

---

At some point, things will fall apart.

---

So much of startup life is simply surviving yet another day.

---

No job is below you—including putting dishes in the dishwasher.

---

Art is long, life is short, and success is very far off.

C2MF

# Book Recommendations

## LEADERSHIP STRATEGY

*Setting the Table: The Transforming Power of Hospitality in Business* by Danny Meyer. My favorite business book, hands down. Danny Meyer is an icon in the New York City restaurant industry, spanning fine dining (Gramercy Tavern, Union Square Café) through to his smaller passion projects (Blue Smoke, Shake Shack). He has set the stage for high standards and expectations regarding delivery to customers across all his endeavors.

*The Founder's Dilemmas: Anticipating and Avoiding the Pitfalls That Can Sink a Startup* by Noam Wasserman. The OG of startup founder support books. It is so substantial and thorough that I can only hope that my own perspectives in my writing project can help to update some of its principles. I am truly standing on the shoulders of giants.

*Mastering the Rockefeller Habits: What You Must Do to Increase the Value of Your Growing Firm* by Verne Harnish. A direct, hands-on framework to define and follow the steps needed to grow your firm (including the BHAG). I found this volume immensely valuable in helping you to build out your company's growth planning for the medium term (before you become a scale-up).

*Never Split the Difference: Negotiating as If Your Life Depended on It* by Christopher Voss, Tahl Raz. Similar in many ways to Dr. Robert Cialdini's "Influence," this volume is particularly valuable as a resource to prepare yourself for the best tactics during negotiations (and to be armed with a defense against people who've also read the book and wish to use it against *you*).

*Radical Candor: Be a Kick-Ass Boss without Losing Your Humanity* by Kim Scott. Often unfairly maligned to its misappropriation by jerks, this book helps to set the appropriate tone to your interactions so that criticism is constructive rather than hurtful.

## PERSONAL DEVELOPMENT/PSYCHOLOGY

*No Fears, No Excuses: What You Need to Do to Have a Great Career* by Larry Smith. My favorite professor from university (ECON 101/102) always promoted the postulate that you'd truly better love what you do, or you'll eventually need to address this with regret. The core within this book helps one to identify what you are passionate about—with the caveat that ideally you need to extend that to what is valuable to the outside world as well.

*Influence: The Psychology of Persuasion* by Dr. Robert Cialdini. The seminal text detailing principles of persuasion. Not only valuable within a sales context, but as building your own personal defense when the tactics are used against you. You'll never look at anyone's marketing program the same after you read this book.

*The Resilient Founder: Lessons in Endurance from Startup Entrepreneurs* by Mahendra Ramsinghani. A warm yet prescriptive text addressing the seldom-addressed aspects of personal resilience and mental fortitude for founders including impulse control, introspection, and awareness.

*The Creative Act: A Way of Being* by Rick Rubin. As a founder, you may find yourself creating something that simply did not exist before. Renaissance man/Zen Buddhist Rick Rubin helps to codify the creative process and discuss inspiration, purpose, and collaboration. If those aren't essential facets of the founder's journey, I simply don't know what are.

## SALES AND STRATEGY

*Founding Sales* by Peter Kazanjy. An incredibly thorough treatment of the founder-led sales process. It cannot be overstated how valuable and topical this reference is to the first-time salesperson (including you, the founder, who may have been pushed kicking and screaming into this role). This book helps to explain what is required of founders to drive sales at each step of the way and gives specific examples regarding how to build sales playbooks, teams, and scalable sales processes.

*Mastering Technical Sales: The Sales Engineer's Handbook* by John Care. The gold standard for technical sales engineers, detailing how best to create a bridge between technical details and the commercial interests necessary to support direct sales personnel.

*UP and to the RIGHT: Strategy and Tactics of Analyst Influence* by Richard Stiennon. The best book to help understand the world of analysts (such as Gartner and Forrester) and what it takes to get their attention. If you're playing in the world of tech, sooner or later, you'll need to get a better sense of who your competition is and where you rank when compared to them. The analyst firms excel at pigeonholing how you are perceived by others, so it's critical that you learn how to position yourself in the best possible light.

## VENTURE/FUNDRAISING

*A Practical Guide to Angel Investing* by Steven A. Gedeon, PhD. I figure that if you'll be pitching to angel investors, you should get a sense as to what they're looking for. This slim volume provides a rapid education into how angel investors should structure their portfolios to achieve good returns. You can use this information to make your startup look more attractive to them.

*Venture Deals: Be Smarter Than Your Lawyer and Your Venture Capitalist* by Brad Feld and Jason Mendelson. The *Bible* for founders trying to make sense of venture capital strategy and structure. Despite the title, after reading this book, you likely won't become smarter than either your lawyer or your VC (who, let's face it, undoubtedly have spent more time on these deals), but you will better understand most of the intricacies within the venture capital process.

*Exit Right: How to Sell Your Startup, Maximize Your Return, and Build Your Legacy* by Mark Achler and Mert Iseri. A superb companion to *Venture Deals*, specifically by laying out a framework of goals through extending a founder's vision within a structure aligned to the long-term horizon—setting yourself up for success from the very beginning.

I have found that these books have so much rich and valuable advice, but some of the advice given may contradict others. As I've said previously, take all advice with a fist-sized grain of salt. You might find that the more specific the advice is, the more likely that it will become outdated quickly. Strategies that work within product-focused companies may not work as well within service-oriented companies (and vice versa). Your mileage may vary.

# Index